CO-024 S

t.f.h.

TARANTULAS

A COMPLETE INTRODUCTION

The bright leg colors of this Brachypelma smithi *indicate that the specimen is an adult.*

A gorgeous specimen of the Mexican Red-leg Tarantula, Brachypelma smithi, *the species favored by many keepers.*

CONTENTS

PHOTO CREDITS

Dr. Herbert R. Axelrod; Dr. Guido Dingerkus; P.A. Federsoni; Isabelle Francais; Michael Gilroy; Alex Kerstitch; Ken Lucas, Steinhart Aquarium; C.O. Masters; Dr. Sherman A. Minton; Alcide Perucca; Ron Reagan; Ivan Sazima.

Distributed in the UNITED STATES by T.F.H. Publications, Inc., 211 West Sylvania Avenue, Neptune City, NJ 07753; in CANADA to the Pet Trade by H & L Pet Supplies Inc., 27 Kingston Crescent, Kitchener, Ontario N2B 2T6; Rolf C. Hagen Ltd., 3225 Sartelon Street, Montreal 382 Quebec; in CANADA to the Book Trade by Macmillan of Canada (A Division of Canada Publishing Corporation), 164 Commander Boulevard, Agincourt, Ontario M1S 3C7; in ENGLAND by T.F.H. Publications Limited, 4 Kier Park, Ascot, Berkshire SL5 7DS; in AUSTRALIA AND THE SOUTH PACIFIC by T.F.H. (Australia) Pty. Ltd., Box 149, Brookvale 2100 N.S.W., Australia; in NEW ZEALAND by Ross Haines & Son, Ltd., 18 Monmouth Street, Grey Lynn, Auckland 2 New Zealand; in SINGAPORE AND MALAYSIA by MPH Distributors (S) Pte., Ltd., 601 Sims Drive, #03/07/21, Singapore 1438; in the PHILIPPINES by Bio-Research, 5 Lippay Street, San Lorenzo Village, Makati Rizal; in SOUTH AFRICA by Multipet Pty. Ltd., 30 Turners Avenue, Durban 4001. Published by T.F.H. Publications Inc. Manufactured in the United States of America by T.F.H. Publications, Inc.

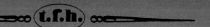

TARANTULAS

A COMPLETE INTRODUCTION

An inactive Trinidad Tarantula, Tepemechenius plumipes. The presence of a web and a still-living cricket indicates possible pre-molting behavior.

Al David

Introduction

Many people appear to have an instinctive dislike of spiders, yet such is the bizarre fascination of these creatures that they nevertheless exert a unique attraction. Indeed, although tarantulas may not be at the top of everyone's favorite pet list, there is no doubt that they are becoming highly popular as pets in domestic surroundings. Furthermore, these spiders are not difficult creatures to keep in the home and require relatively little attention. Pet tarantulas, apart from being a subject of conversation with friends and neighbors and at parties, also afford their owners a unique opportunity to study these maligned creatures at close quarters. A considerable amount of information about tarantulas has become available through the observations of enthusiasts based on study of their pets. Although potential owners may initially be attracted to a tarantula by virture of its reputation, they are soon likely to become fully engrossed by the interesting behavior of these large spiders. The sinister reputation of the tarantula dates back centuries. In Europe, spiders were believed to be responsible for a serious disease (curable only by wild dancing) that was known as *tarantism.* Named after the town of Tarantum in Italy, where the legend appears to have developed, the mania spread throughout Europe in the Middle Ages. Large spiders that were being discovered in ever increasing numbers as European travelers entered tropical areas soon also came to be viewed as a source of danger, and thus further legends surrounding the spiders loosely called "tarantulas" began to evolve. These are still prevalent today in most parts of the world. Modern representations of tarantulas, in films and television especially, have done little to enlighten people about the true life styles of these essentially shy spiders. The situation also has not been helped by confusion over the proper names for the different groups of spiders. It was in fact the European wolf spider (*Lycosa tarantula*) that gave rise to the tarantism mania and the popular superstitions about "tarantulas" in Italy. Although a burrowing species, these spiders are not in fact close relatives of the tarantulas sold in pet stores, which belong to a different family. Even among relatively educated people any large spider is likely to be called a tarantula and assumed to be dangerous. That this is not so should be obvious to anyone who reads this book. Perhaps someday tarantulas will be able to take their rightful place as simply large, fascinating spiders.

To the modern terrarium keeper, the tarantula is an object of fascination, not fear. These large, even spectacular, spiders have become available in good variety of late. As hobbyists learn more about them, they survive longer under captive conditions and can now even be bred commercially on a small scale.

What is a Tarantula?

Spiders of course have a wide distribution throughout the world, and there are over 30,000 species recognized by scientists. Tarantulas are the largest members of this group and are classified in the suborder Orthognatha (formerly Mygalomorpha), which is divided into a number of minor and major families. Members of the Ctenizidae, for example, are known as trap-door spiders because their burrows are sealed and remain hidden to passing prey until the tarantula suddenly emerges to drag the unsuspecting cricket or beetle down.

The tarantulas that hobbyists are interested in form the family Theraphosidae. They are active hunters by nature and usually do not spin webs to catch their prey, although like other spiders they feed largely upon other invertebrates. The food is caught alive and killed by means of venom injected into the body to rapidly stun or kill it. Some tarantulas are called bird-eating spiders, but none of the 300 or more species in this family feeds predominantly on vertebrates. They may on occasion catch and consume a small bird, however, seizing a tiny nestling if the occasion presents itself, and some are able to subdue small lizards on a regular basis. Crickets, grasshoppers, beetles, flies, and roaches are much more normal prey.

Their opportunistic natures make them easy to cater for in domestic surroundings, and species labelled "bird-eaters" can be kept quite satisfactorily on a diet comprised exclusively of invertebrates. Some members of the group do tend to be more aggressive than others, though, and this can be significant when choosing a pet. The biggest member of the group is found in northern parts of South America and is often known as the Goliath Bird Spider (*Theraphosa leblondi*). Weighing about 3 ounces, males of this species can have a leg span in excess of 10 inches. They are rarely available to the tarantula enthusiast, however, and invariably command a high price.

While New World species are best known in captivity, members of this family have a wide distribution through tropical and subtropical areas of the world. Their coloration can be quite variable, although the majority of species tend to be relatively dull in appearance, essentially brownish or black overall.

Structure

The tarantulas show features common to all spiders but also have several unique charateristics that set them apart in their own family. Arachnids, as spiders, scorpions, mites, and their allies are collectively known, are members of the class Arachnida and are not insects (class Insecta). Spiders possess eight legs compared with the six of the insects, the most obvious distinguishing character. Their body is confined in a rigid casing known as an exoskeleton. As the spider grows it must undergo sequential molts, gaining a progressively larger exoskeleton each time. Serious damage to the exoskeleton can have fatal consequences for the spider,

This Pink-toed Tarantula, Avicularia avicularia, *is hairier than most other species available in the hobby. It is one of the arboreal (tree-dwelling) species.*

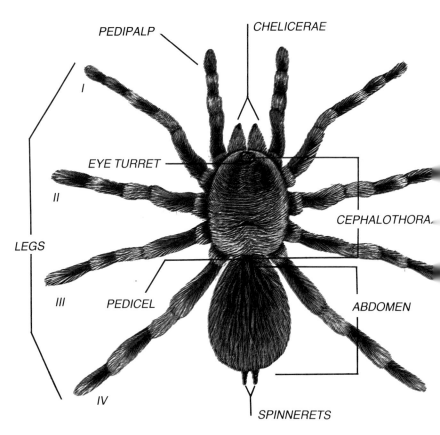

PEDIPALP

CHELICERAE

EYE TURRET

CEPHALOTHORA.

LEGS

I

II

III

IV

PEDICEL

ABDOMEN

SPINNERETS

Dorsal view of a typical tarantula, showing the major sections of the body and the major appendages. All tarantulas are very much alike in structure, which is one of the reasons they are almost impossible to identify to genus and species.

and they need to be handled carefully for this reason, although some degree of natural repair (such as regeneration of legs) is possible.

The body of a tarantula is in two distinct sections (cephalothorax, abdomen) instead of the three sections characteristic of insects (head, thorax, abdomen). The head and thorax are fused together, forming the front segment known as the cephalothorax, which is in turn connected to the abdominal segment of the body. There is a link between the two segments formed by the pedicel. The exoskeleton over the abdomen is thinner, rendering the spider more vulnerable to injury at this point yet permitting some expansion in body size, as for example when the female is ready to breed and her abdomen swells with eggs.

The legs of the tarantula are paired and originate under the cephalothorax, almost always with two pairs pointing in a forward direction and two pairs pointing back. Between the front pair of legs the "palps" or "pedipalps" can be seen. These look like legs but attach to the head region rather than further back as do the true legs. The palps serve as a means of distinguishing the sexes and can also be useful in recognizing different species. They are more highly developed in males, being used for mating purposes.

Ventral view of a tarantula, showing the major sections of the body and major appendages. This is a female because the pedipalps end bluntly, without a darkened process, and there are no hooks on the femurs of the first legs.

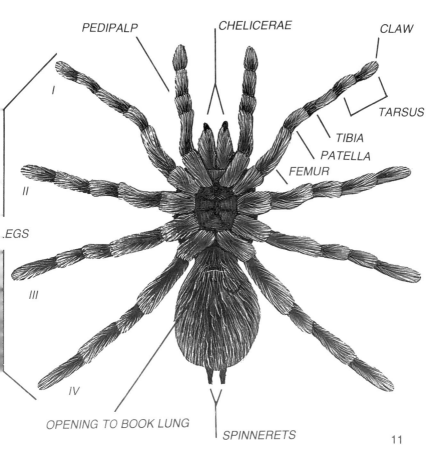

11

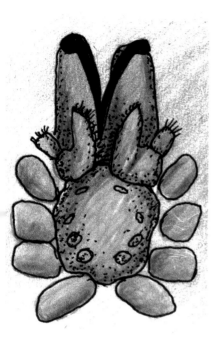

Diagram of the chelicerae and anterior part of the body of a tarantula from beneath, showing the almost parallel, downwardly thursting fangs (in black).

spiders that serves to distinguish them as a more primitive group when compared with their web-spinning cousins is the arrangement of their jaws. The thrust is in a downward direction, enabling the prey to be trapped firmly against the ground so the venom can be injected without difficulty from poison glands at the base of the chelicerae.

Chelicerae

The tarantula's eyes are clearly visible on the top of its head. Below the front pair the mouthparts, known as the chelicerae (singular, chelicera), will be evident. These claw-like jaws are used to inject prey with venom, a fang being present for this purpose at the end of the chelicera. One of the characteristics of the orthognath (mygalomorph)

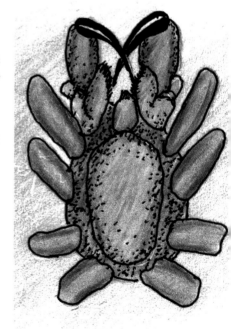

Diagram of the chelicerae and anterior part of the body of an advanced spider from beneath, showing the crossed, horizontally thrusting fangs (in black).

This approach is not likely to be so reliable in spiders sitting in a web, such as the majority of "higher" or web-spinning spiders, which may have no firm surface available to them against which prey could be restrained for this

Cross-section through a chelicera of a tarantula, showing the fang (in black) and the sac-like poison gland fitting into the base of the fang (the gland has been pulled to the right to show it better).

purpose. In these species the chelicerae are no longer directed vertically downward, but they have evolved to become more widely spaced, their tips pointing horizontally inward so that prey can be seized more easily.

The chelicerae have a mechanical function in addition to dispensing venom, serving to manipulate food (in conjunction with other mouthparts) toward the mouth. In some species the chelicerae are more serrated, with additional combs of teeth (usually toward the forward outer edge) being used to facilitate the excavation of burrows where the spiders can conceal themselves. Study has shown that Old World species of tarantulas in particular can also use these teeth and similar structures that may be present on the palps nearby to make a sudden rasping noise if they are startled or threatened by a predator. Described as stridulation, the actual significance of this action is unclear, but it may be a defensive response toward the perceived danger.

Defensive techniques

The hairy appearance of the tarantulas offers an excellent line of defense, since the "hairs," which are in fact bristles, may have an irritating effect on any creature that ventures too close to the spider. They are frequently tipped with glassy barbs and break off from the spider's body very easily, especially over the top of the abdomen where a predator is

The raised abdomen of this Brazilian *Pamphobeteus tetracanthus* shows that it is ready to defend itself by rubbing stinging or urticating hairs from the top of the abdomen. This is the main defense of most American tarantulas.

most likely to strike. Various distinctive types of these *urticating hairs* have been identified, some of which are equipped with barbs directed forward. These will penetrate to a pre-determined depth and also prove difficult to remove. Close contact with a tarantula around an animal's head will frequently lead to bouts of sneezing and cause severe eye irritation. This distraction should then enable the tarantula to escape.

Clearly this means of defense must be appreciated by tarantula keepers because humans can be affected in a similar way. The effects of the urticating bristles are more likely to be encountered following careless handling than is a bite from the spider in question. In any event, you should never encourage the tarantula to climb over your body, since if by any chance it falls to the ground the impact could split its abdomen open and may well prove fatal.

As a general rule, New World tarantulas are preferred as pets, being more tractable than Old World species. It is interesting that these spiders as a group are better protected by urticating bristles and apparently as part of the tarantula's nervous system. These are extremely sensitive, with a nerve impulse being detectable experimentally if just a single bristle is touched lightly. Other similar sensory devices over the body surface

The so-called Red-rumped Tarantula is an attractive species recognized by the abdomen being covered with long red hairs. The absence of a bald spot in this specimen indicates that it has recently molted. The scientific name is unknown, as is true of most tarantulas in the hobby.

cannot stridulate in the same way as their Old World counterparts. Old World tarantulas are relatively aggressive, possibly because they are not so well protected when directly threatened by a potential predator.

Senses

Specialized bristles also act include trichobothria, which are fine hairs that respond even to the air disturbance caused by an insect such as a cricket or fly nearby. These probably have a key role in locating prey.

The eyes themselves are of very little significance in locating prey, serving primarily to detect differences in light intensity,

Although the bite of most tarantulas is nearly harmless, there are some species that are truly venomous and dangerous to man. Tarantulas of the genus Atrax *(in a different family from the common hobby tarantulas) are common in Australia and have on occasion caused human deaths. An antivenin is available.*

although in two families of spiders, the net-casting spiders (Dinopidae), also known as the ogre-eyed spiders, and the jumping spiders (Salticidae), acute vision is vital to their survival and their eyes are very well developed.

The center of the spider's nervous system is located close to the lower part of the cephalothorax, linking with the internal organs and external limbs. A large nerve trunk also passes via the pedicel into the abdomen, linking this part of the body with the brain.

Blood supply

The circulatory system of tarantulas and other spiders differs significantly from that of higher vertebrates. The heart pumps the blood around the arteries into the body tissues. It is located near the top of the abdomen in the midline and takes the form of a tube, with blood entering by means of four pairs of openings described as ostia. From here blood passes forward via the pedicel, being released to the tissues present in the cephalothorax. It does not enter a series of ever-smaller vessels, as in mammals for example, but flows freely through the body cavities in direct contact with the tissues. The venous system is then responsible for circulating blood back into the abdomen, where it passes through the book lungs and gains oxygen before being returned to the arterial circulation by the heart. The blood collects first in the covering of the heart, the pericardium.

Book lungs
The tarantula equivalents of lungs are located in the abdomen, being clearly visible when the spider is viewed from below. These book lungs are seen as hairless patches, rather reminiscent of pockets when studied in detail, and can vary in number among the various families. In the case of tarantulas and related spiders there generally are

two pairs visible. Internally the lungs resemble the open pages of a book, being comprised of a series of folds. Through these thin membranes gaseous exchange takes place as blood is pumped through them by heart beats. Between the leaves air is present, and here carbon dioxide diffuses out of the body and oxygen is absorbed.

Diagram of a tarantula's abdomen from below, showing the openings to the two pairs of book lungs.

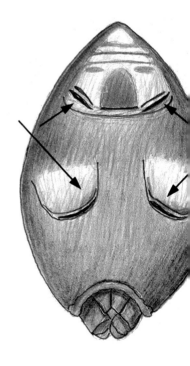

What is a Tarantula?

The book lungs are not without disadvantages, however. The spider is not able to breathe in the vertebrate sense, and the system is unable to supply increased amounts of oxygen when required, since gas transfer appears to be a passive process controlled by the rate of diffusion for the gases concerned. In addition, while under normal circumstances book lungs provide an adequate medium for gaseous exchange to take place, they also enable a not inconsiderable amount of water to be lost from the body by evaporation at the same time.

These factors were probably responsible for the gradual modification of the book lungs into tracheae in some spiders, although this change is not seen in tarantulas, providing further

Diagram of a tarantula's book lung. The thin plates of membrane allow intake of oxygen and release of carbon dioxide. A tarantula cannot actively breathe like a mammal or even a fish.

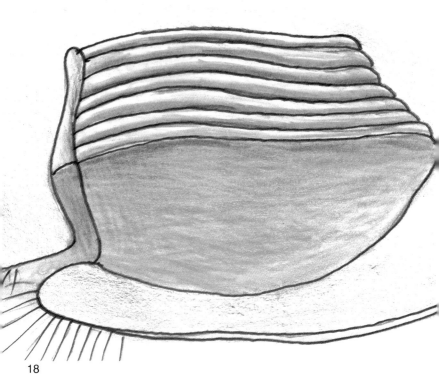

Because the exchange of carbon dioxide for oxygen in the book lung takes place relatively slowly, a tarantula is seldom an active animal. Also, under conditions of low atmospheric humidity much water vapor is lost from the body through evaporation, resulting in dehydration.

evidence of their relatively primitive status. In cases where tracheae are present, they serve to admit atmospheric oxygen directly into the body cavity.

Oxygen transport in the blood is carried out by red blood cells in vertebrates, but no specialized cells exist for this function within the spider's circulatory system. Indeed, instead of hemoglobin, which is used to bind oxygen reversibly in the vertebrate system, spiders rely on a different pigment, hemocyanin, containing copper rather than iron, for the purpose. Instead of being linked with individual cells, the pigment circulates freely within the blood or hemolymph, as it is more scientifically described. It is because of the presence of hemocyanin that a spider's hemolymph appears pale bluish rather than red when viewed against a suitable background. Under normal circumstances, however, it shows little color.

Several distinctive types of cells have been identified in the hemolymph, and these appear to have the same functions as the white cell populations present in vertebrate blood. They therefore probably help to prevent infections and assist in the clotting of hemolymph if the external protective cuticle is damaged. Interestingly, all the cells in the hemolymph appear to originate from the heart wall, being released directly into the circulation from here, so the heart is doubly vital to the spider.

Digestive processes

Predigestion is essential in the case of tarantulas, which, like other spiders, are unable to swallow their prey whole. Their small mouth, visible between the pedipalps on the lower surface of the body, is positioned directly in front of the protrusion of the sternum known as the labium. This forms a type of lower lip, with the labrum or upper lip being located near the base of the chelicerae. Instead of using muscular jaws to macerate

their prey, tarantulas rely on their external limbs close to the mouth to undertake this task, the bases of the pedipalps and first legs often being toothed or knobby to help maceration.

Digestive fluid containing enzymes that begin the digestive process is passed out of the mouth into and onto the prey. The resulting solution of partially digested prey containing dissolved nutrients is drawn back through the mouth by the action of the tarantula's sucking stomach. This organ, which is found at the terminus of the esophagus, is under the control of muscles that attach to the walls of the cephalothorax. There are numerous hairs present within the mouth and neighboring pharynx that serve to filter the ingesta, removing minute particles of food and other debris that may have been swallowed accidentally. This ensures that only fluid is passed into the lower part of the digestive tract, with the retained particles being flushed out of the mouth by regurgitation of digestive juices from the sucking stomach.

A system of valves located in the sucking stomach then ensures that the ingesta is able to move through to the remainder of the intestinal tract. The true stomach of the tarantula is located within the cephalothorax close to the brain, beyond the sucking stomach. Absorption of nutrients actually appears to take place in the next section of the tract, which is known as the midgut. Here additional enzymes are concerned.

The posterior part of the gut is known as the hindgut and ends in the cloacal chamber. Here solid fecal waste from the digestive process is stored prior to being excreted from the body. Spiders produce guanine as an unwanted

Tarantulas are primarily "lurking" animals, lying in wait for prey to come by their retreat. Specimens in captivity will spend most of their time under cover of a piece of bark or flowerpot, resting in a shallow burrow.

released so that the nutrients already in solution can be broken down further, enabling them to be absorbed into the spider's body. In order to facilitate this process, the midgut has a large surface area expanded by sacs known as diverticula that serve to increase the efficiency of the process. The diverticula can occupy a large area within the abdomen, depending to some extent on the species metabolic by-product, whereas nitrogenous wastes in most other creatures are excreted mainly as ammonia or a closely related compound.

Tarantulas have coxal glands that may have an excretory function. These can be identified in the cephalothorax and connect to pores present on the first and third coxae. When the tarantula is viewed from beneath, the coxae themselves are clearly visible as the first leg segments, ringing the cephalothorax.

Movement

It is by means of the coxae that the tarantula's legs attach to the body. The coxa is the first of the seven segments that constitute each leg. These are held together by hinged joints. Much of the cephalothorax is comprised of muscle tissue responsible for moving the legs. Each individual leg may be controlled by as many as 30 separate muscles. The limb segments are all known under individual names: The *trochanter* connects between the *coxa* and *femur*, which in turn links the *patella*, which then joins the *tibia*. The *tarsus* may appear to be comprised of two further segments, but in reality the two components, sometimes described as the *basitarsus* and *telotarsus*, are not under independent muscle control and therefore not truly segmented. The most distal segment from the ccphalothorax is the *pretarsus*, more often called the *claw*. These limb segments correspond to those of the pedipalps.

The presence of hemolymph is crucial to the spider's mobility, since this enables the joints to be extended. The muscles themselves serve just to retract the legs, whereas the pressure of the hemolymph ensures the spider's mobillty

This close-up of the patella of a Mexican Red-leg shows how the color is restricted mostly to one type of hair. The longer hairs have sensory functions.

Facing Page: *The relative lengths of the different leg joints vary considerably from one type of tarantula to another.* Tapemechenius plumipes.

If you look carefully, you can see that this Red-rumped Tarantula has produced several strands of silk. Unlike most spiders, tarantulas usually build webs only for special purposes rather than for catching prey.

via the joints. This system places immediate constraints on the spider's size, however, since as it becomes heavier the pressure needed to lift its limbs increases dramatically. Measurements have suggested that some spiders have a hemolymph pressure in excess of human blood pressure, in spite of the relatively primitive structure of their circulatory system. The actual loss of a limb usually is not a serious handicap to a spider, and regeneration is possible.

Silk

At least seven different types of silk can be produced by spiders from different types of silk glands located in the abdomen. Although tarantulas do not construct a traditional web, they will use silk for wrapping prey that they will subsequently eat. This is produced by the aciniform glands. Females also have cylindrical glands that produce the silk that forms their egg sacs. The silk itself is a form of protein with considerable strength and elasticity. It actually leaves the spider's body as a liquid via the *spinnerets.* These small projections are responsible for stretching the silk, which in turn causes it to become solidified. Furthermore, its chemical characteristics are altered by this process, rendering it insoluble in water. Some species of spiders have developed highly sophisticated webs for catching prey. Orb web spiders (*Araneus*), for example, can produce as much as 765 yards of silk in a single thread.

Classification and Selection

Tarantulas, in view of their sedentary habits, are ideal spiders to keep in the home. Much new information about these distinctive and rather primitive spiders has already become available from the observations of their keepers, and several active societies are flourishing in various parts of the world, providing the very latest information through their journals.

You may possibly think that it is rather off-beat to keep a spider as a pet. Tarantulas will not become tame in the same way as will a parrot, for example, but they will provide a constant source of fascination and interest. They are not difficult to maintain, and there is always the possibility that a

Because the taxonomy of tarantulas is very unsettled, it is usually impossible to give a meaningful scientific name to a specimen purchased commercially. Most tarantulas could be called big brown to black spiders, as few show distinctive patterns. Brachypelma smithi *is an exception.*

pair may be encouraged to mate successfully, with the hatching and rearing of young spiderlings in the home now becoming an increasingly common event. It is easy to keep a number of tarantulas even in a small apartment where other, more conventional pets would be outlawed. They will not disturb the neighbors, yet they provide a unique link with the broader, natural world in the face of an increasingly urbanized society.

Choosing your tarantula

Many pet stores have tarantulas for sale, although the choice of species available may be rather limited. There are specialist suppliers, however, who usually have a much wider selection, although it might prove necessary to purchase stock unseen if they are based some distance away. It may be possible to have the spider sent by mail, but check with the supplier and the post office first to ensure that no postal regulations would be violated if this route were used. It is generally best to select the spider in person so you can choose the individual that you want.

There are various health pointers that need to be considered in this respect.

Obviously, it is preferable to opt for an individual with a plump appearance. A sickly-looking spider may not in fact be ill, but could simply be dehydrated. Tarantulas do lose fluid from their bodies, notably via their book lungs, and this loss must be made good. Although they can survive for months without drinking, it is best to offer a shallow dish of water to a new arrival right from the outset.

Sexual differences

Individuals that are lacking a limb or two generally command a lower price than complete animals, and while regeneration may take place over successive molts during the course of several years, this is unlikely to occur in the case of male tarantulas. Their lives tend to be much shorter than those of their female counterparts. It is possible to recognize mature males by the presence of finger-like hooks evident on the femoral section of their first pair of legs. The pedipalps of males also become enlarged and swollen at their tips for breeding purposes.

A difference in temperament is similarly likely to be apparent: mature males are extremely restless and at this stage in the wild wander most persistently in search of potential mates. They are then more conspicuous and likely to be caught. It is not surprising, therefore, that a relatively high proportion of the tarantulas available in pet stores tend to be mature males with a subsequent maximum life expectancy of perhaps only a year.

While much still remains to be learned about the life hidden in burrows, and they are thus far less commonly available.

Although concern has been expressed about the number of North American tarantulas being traded, especially the Mexican Red-leg (*Brachypelma smithi*), there is no real evidence to show that at present overall populations are being adversely affected. The males in the trade are in

In many ways the name tarantula is a misnomer. Not only is it involved with a European wolf spider, but the animal that bears the generic name Tarantula *is not even a spider. Shown is the true* Tarantula, *a tailless whipscorpion that is only indirectly related to the spiders.*

cycles of the individual species, it does seem that few males naturally survive the winter period in the United States, although this does depend to some extent on when they hatched and subsequently attained maturity. Female tarantulas, in contrast, may live for over a decade, remaining largely effect largely irrelevant to maintaining the species's numbers, since they are nearing the end of their lifespans. Damage to the burrows where colonies of females and immatures occur, however, could inflict serious harm on the total population of a region in a short space of time.

Monitoring of the situation is required, and this has at least been achieved in part by the transfer of the Mexican Red-leg to Appendix II status under the internationally accepted CITES agreement. This serves to regulate trade by means of a permit system when these tarantulas are moved from country to country.

In the future, it seems likely that the demand for tarantulas will be met increasingly from captive-bred stock as it becomes more routine for these spiders to reproduce successfully under captive conditions. Indeed, commercial breeding could potentially prove quite lucrative, since females can produce a huge number of eggs.

Classification of tarantulas

It is of course important to be able to identify and thus describe a particular tarantula with certainty. The basic system used for this purpose does not differ from that employed in other areas of the animal kingdom. As long ago as the 4th Century, the Greek philosopher Aristotle devised a means of identifying related creatures and placing them in groups. Although various aspects of this system were retained,

classification today stems essentially from the 18th Century scheme devised by Linnaeus, who relied more on anatomical similarities in a visual rather than a functional sense.

Linnaeus's method operates via a series of ranks that become progressively more specific (narrower) as the groupings become smaller. Although scientific names may seem an unnecessary complication, they provide the only reliable means of distinguishing between various tarantulas in written or spoken words. The common names of these spiders are not well-established and simply tend to reflect obvious characteristics that are shared with many other spiders, and indeed even other tarantulas. As an example, in the following section there are two so-called Zebra Tarantulas that both have striped markings. They are not closely related, however, and when given just the information of the common name the prospective purchaser is likely to be uncertain as to which species he will be acquiring.

All spiders are classified in the class Arachnida. The example of the Central American Zebra Tarantula

An Acanthoscurria *species from Argentina. Identification of tarantulas requires careful examination of proportions, hair patterns, and sexual organs.*

shows the various ranks within the classificatory system:

Class: Arachnida; Order: Araneae; Suborder: Orthognatha; Family: Theraphosidae; Subfamily: Grammostolinae; Genus: *Aphonopelma*; Species: *Aphonopelma seemanni*; Describer: (Cambridge); Year of Description: 1897.

Classification is not a static discipline, and changes, especially at the level of the species, are not uncommon as new information becomes available. In this instance a change of generic classification has occurred since the species was first described in 1897. This can be ascertained by the fact that the name of the person who described this species—Cambridge—is placed in parenthesis. The number of species of tarantulas grouped in the family Theraphosidae presently totals in excess of 650 and will doubtless be expanded still further as others are discovered in various parts of the world. The first species to be classified was in fact the giant of the family, popularly known as the **Goliath Bird Spider (*Theraphosa leblondi*)**, which was described as long ago as 1804.

Classification and Selection

Tarantula subfamilies

It is obviously not possible to consider every species of tarantula in this book. Many are virtually unknown in captivity, so relatively little has been recorded about their habits. This section reviews all six subfamilies that comprise the family Theraphosidae. From this it is possible to gain some insight into the relationships among the various genera that follow in the next section. Classification of all spiders, including tarantulas, is being based increasingly on the anatomical appearance of the genital organs, and as this standard becomes more widely applied to members of these various subfamilies revisions to existing taxonomy will become almost inevitable.

Subfamily Grammostolinae

This is the most significant subfamily for the tarantula enthusiast, since the majority of the species available belong to this group. All 17 genera are confined to the New World, with the majority of species being found in the United States and Central America, although others occur as far south as parts of Chile. Such popular genera as *Brachypelma, Aphonopelma, Dugesiella, Grammostola*, and *Eurypelma* all feature

Although sold as the Orange-knee Tarantula under the name Aphono-pelma emiliae, *there is no guarantee that this is the correct scientific name. Fortunately for hobbyists, most tarantulas do well under roughly similar conditions regardless of their names.*

Grammostola actaeon *from South America. This is a far-southern relative of the familiar Mexican Red-leg.*

under this heading. Given the wide distribution of this subfamily, some species will need to be maintained at higher humidity levels than others. Those from North America tend to require a figure around 65% RH (occurring as they do in relatively arid areas), compared with those species found in tropical rain forests that need to be kept in conditions where the humidity reading is held at about 80%.

Subfamily Aviculariinae The name "Aviculariidae" was used as a family name for the so-called bird-eating spiders until well into the present century. Since then, however, it has been down-graded to subfamily status as Aviculariinae. The earliest recorded report of spiders eating birds can be traced back to a book published during 1705, entitled *Metamorphosis Insectorum Surinamensis.* Here the author, Maria Meren, describes how she witnessed a hummingbird fall victim to a black spider. This tale was accepted and was encapsulated in the generic term *Avicularia*, devised in 1818 and still used today. ***Avicularia avicularia*** is certainly the most common of these bird-eating spiders seen in collections at present and appears to be equally numerous in the wild.

This is a widespread subfamily with representatives also occurring in Africa. The baboon spiders, contained in the genera ***Heteroscodra*** and ***Scodra***, are primarily arboreal, like other members of the subfamily. They are sometimes described as **Stout Hind-legged** and **Feather-legged Baboon Spiders**, respectively. They inhabit tropical forest areas and require suitably humid conditions. The term "baboon spider" is not specific, however, and is applied to other members of the family found in Africa.

the similarity of their legs to the appearance of a primate's digits. These spiders are actually considered to be a popular delicacy in certain parts of their range, being roasted after their poison glands have been removed. Members of the genus ***Ceratogyrus*** are distinctive in possessing a swelling resembling a horn on their upperparts, so they are

The long hairs of the Red-rump Tarantula possibly indicate that it is related to Avicularia, *but this seems to be a ground-dwelling species.*

Subfamily Selenocosmiinae It is usual to split this subfamily into three further subdivisions that are partially geographical in origin. The Harpactireae features other baboon spiders, so-called because of

known as **Horned Baboon Spiders**. The shape of this foveal horn is variable, which helps to distinguish the individual species. This group tends to require slightly lower humidity than the baboon spiders in the subfamily

Aviculariinae.

The two other groups related to the Harpactireae can be found from India to Australasia, but these particular tarantulas are not commonly available to enthusiasts. Some species occur on the islands in this part of the world, such as the **Java Yellow-kneed Tarantula (*Selecocosmia javanensis*)**, whose range includes the Malayan Peninsula, Sumatra, and the Lesser Nicobars, as well as Java itself. Slight differences in this instance are not uncommon as the tarantulas have evolved separately in isolation. The populations from different localities are sometimes given subspecific status, indicated by the addition of a third name after the species name, such as *Selecocosmia javanensis sumatrana*. This reflects their close relationship, yet also serves to show there is a difference between these populations.

Although the bite of the vast majority of tarantulas will not be harmful to humans, a few members of this subfamily can prove poisonous. These include some of the highly colorful members of the Poecilotherieae, which are found in certain parts of India as well as Sri Lanka. In

A Baboon Spider, Harpactirella, *from southern Africa. These spiders have a bad bite.*

addition, the **Bobbejaan Baboon Spider (*Harpactirella lightfooti*)** from southern Africa is known to be poisonous. None of these species are normally available, however, but if in doubt, and certainly in field conditions, avoid placing yourself at risk by attempting to handle such spiders directly.

Subfamily Theraphosinae Another New World group, the Theraphosinae is comprised of 11 genera and features some of the largest known spiders in the world, including the **Goliath Bird Spider (*Theraphosa leblondi*)**. The subfamily is divided into two groups, with this particular species being featured in the Theraphoseae. All these tarantulas require quite humid surroundings, with a relative humidity reading between 70 and 80%. They range through Central and South America, occurring both in rain forests and drier areas, and some species are found in the Caribbean. This group includes members of the genus *Acanthoscurria*, which are most numerous in Brazil.

Among the Lasiodoreae there are also some potentially large spiders. One of the most common species is the **Bahia Scarlet Bird-eater (*Lasiodora klugi*)**, which has been reported to weigh 3 oz. From further north, in parts of Colombia extending to Brazil, the **Giant Colombian Bird-eater (*Megaphobema robusta*)** is found in areas of rain forest.

Subfamily Ornithoctoninae The members of this subfamily are confined to Asia, with the species included in the Thrignopoceae group being found in southwestern parts of India. These are regarded by taxonomists as the least evolved members of the whole family Theraposidae. They need to be kept in humid conditions, being found naturally in parts of the world where monsoon conditions are prevalent. At least one species, the **Coimbatore Brown (*Annandaliella pectinifera*)**, is often discovered in close proximity to ant nests, and these invertebrates may provide a natural food source for these tarantulas.

The second group in this subfamily, the Ornithoctoneae, occurs further east, in Southeast Asia. Members of *Melopoeus* feature in this grouping, but other related tarantulas are rarely imported.

Subfamily Ischnocolinae This is the largest subfamily, comprising approximately 50 genera. The members of the group have a correspondingly wide distribution throughout tropical and subtropical areas of the world, occurring in a wide range of habitats. It is likely that in the course of a major reclassification a number of genera would be removed from this subfamily. As an example, members of the genus *Metriopelma*, including the Costa Rican Tiger and Panther Abdomen species, are presently included under this heading.

Compared to most of the other tarantulas illustrated, this species has relatively slender legs.

Although only reported for the first time during 1982, these species are occasionally available to arachnologists. Their classification is rather confused, however, since a member of the genus *Hapalopus*, popularly called the **Costa Rican Orange-banded Tarantula (*H. pentaloris*)**, appears to be very closely related to the **Costa Rican Sun Tiger Abdomen (*Metriopelma zebratus*)**. Indeed, it has been suggested that they could be simply the same species described under two scientific names!

Available species

A relatively large selection of tarantulas is occasionally available. Species vary in their requirements as they occur naturally in different environments. The following is a list of those species that are likely to be encountered and guidelines for their care. Unfortunately, correct identification can be a problem, especially if the vendor does not know the scientific name of the spider in question (and even experts have a hard time identifying tarantulas). Many tarantulas do not have unique common names, and a simple descriptive term derived from the individual's appearance

will often prove of little value to its identification since species from various localities often appear superficially similar. The most common species can be recognized without too much difficulty, however.

Mexican Red-leg Tarantula (*Brachypelma smithi*):
(Also known under the generic term *Eurypelma*.) This has long been one of the most popular species with tarantula keepers. As its name suggests, it originates in Mexico and can be distinguished by the reddish orange markings on its legs, most noticeable close to the body. The cephalothorax tends to be blackish with a brownish border, while the abdomen is black. Although inhabiting arid areas of desert in the wild, the Red-leg is one of the hardier species and will survive well in a temperature above 70°F. Its accommodations must be devised to allow this species's burrowing habits to be exhibited.

The Mexican Red-leg, now less commonly called the Mexican Red-kneed Tarantula, is one of the bigger examples of this group of spiders and may have a leg span of 6 inches. This species is now encountered for sale rather less often than

The Mexican Red-leg Tarantula, Brachypelma smithi. *The color deepens with maturity.*

formerly, but suitable breeding stock can still be obtained. Young offspring will almost certainly find a ready market because of the burden of paperwork placed on importers of wild-collected specimens.

Mexican Blonde Tarantula (*Brachypelma chalcodes*):
(Also known as *Eurypelma* and *Aphonopelma chalcodes*.) This species is popularly referred to as the Mexican Blonde, although these tarantulas are also found in southwestern parts of the United States. If you decide to catch your own,

check that you will not be infringing any laws by so doing. Adequate protection is essential when out seeking tarantulas, against both sharp vegetation and venomous creatures, notably snakes, that are likely to inhabit the same region. The best time to search for tarantulas is during the spring and summer, as they will be more inclined to venture from their burrows at this time of year. During the early fall they tend to be molting and remain in their burrows, where they will spend the winter, becoming relatively inactive until the temperature

The Texas Brown, Dugesiella hentzi, *is common eastward almost up to the Mississippi River. Males are often found wandering on highways.*

An unidentified tarantula, possibly an Aphonopelma, *from Mexico.*

warms up again in the spring.

The Mexican Blonde not surprisingly requires a similar environment to that of its Red-leg relative. It also provides an ideal introduction to the hobby of tarantula keeping, being generally easy to handle when necessary, although it is smaller and not as colorful as the Red-leg. The Mexican Blonde tends to be rather variable in coloration, in fact ranging from shades of fawn through to brown. Other similar species are found in the same area, including the **Texas Brown** *(Dugesiella hentzi),* occurring in various

southwestern states, and the **Rio Grande Gold** *(Aphonopelma heterops),* which tends to be lighter in color as its name suggests. Identical conditions as recommended for the Red-leg will suit these spiders well.

Various tarantulas from the Caribbean region are occasionally available. These include the **Haitian Tarantula** *(Phormictopus cancerides),* which is dull brown in color with a pink cast to its body most noticeable on the cephalothorax. This species requires it be kept at a slightly higher temperature than the North American spiders, around 80°F, and will benefit from a larger enclosure, being more active by nature. Inhabiting a tropical area, it should also be kept under conditions of higher humidity. Although Haitian Tarantulas are not expensive, they tend to be relatively difficult to handle and will frequently attempt to bite if given an opportunity. They are thus not entirely suitable for the novice owner, especially since their management requirements are more demanding than those of preceding species.

The **Pink-toed Tarantula** *(Avicularia avicularia)* is found both on the island of Trinidad and in northern South America, ranging from Guyana to Brazil. It differs significantly in its habits from the previous species, since it is arboreal by nature and has correspondingly larger legs. In common with other essentially tree-dwelling tarantulas, the Pink-toed is relatively nervous but can become quite tame once established in its quarters.

The body of this species is blackish, with a variable degree of iridescence apparent on the cephalothorax. The common name of the Pink-toed is derived from the pinkish tips of its limbs, extending up to the tarsus. This coloration can be quite variable, however, and in some cases it may be orange rather than pink, which almost certainly reflects a regional variation. Further study may even confirm these color forms as being separate species. Their accommodations must be designed to take account of their arboreal habits. Originating close to the Equator, these tarantulas require a temperature around 85°F under conditions of high humidity.

The Pink-toed will often construct a web in its quarters where it will rest with its abdomen pointing upward. Such behavior is quite normal and should not be cause for concern. The Pink-toed is an interesting species that ranks among the least costly of the tarantulas.

Most of the Central American species require similar conditions to the Pink-toed, although not all are arboreal by nature. These include a relative of the Mexican Red-leg known as the **Curly-haired** or **Woolly Honduran Tarantula** *(Brachypelma albopilosa).* This species is characterized by the dense covering of "hairs" present over its body and legs. It tends to be rather subdued in terms of coloration, ranging from

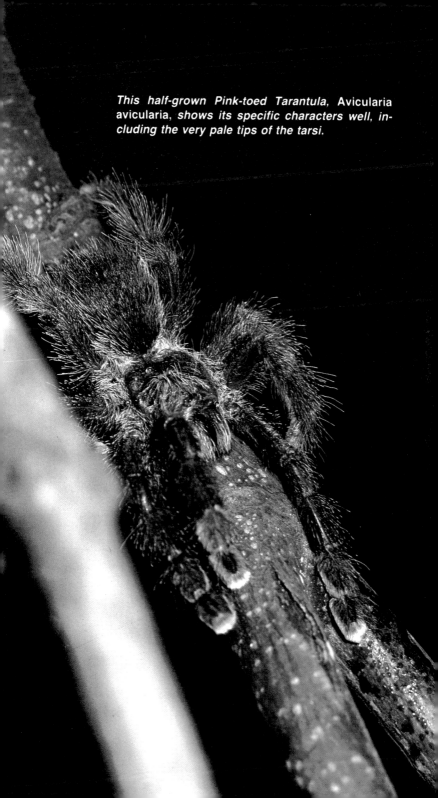

This half-grown Pink-toed Tarantula, Avicularia avicularia, shows its specific characters well, including the very pale tips of the tarsi.

Classification and Selection

black through to brown. Like its more northerly relative, the Curly-haired is a burrowing species. It is sometimes advertised as the **Honduran Black Velvet.**

Several tarantulas from Costa Rica are often available and are basically similar in their requirements. The **Zebra Tarantula (Aphonopelma (Rhecostica) seemanni)** is one of the most attractive species, possessing distinctive light stripes that run the full length of its legs. These pale markings set against the blackish legs have given rise to the common name of this tarantula. Keep this species in a warm, humid environment and provide adequate facilities so that it can burrow. Studies in the wild suggest the maximum depth for these retreats does not exceed 5 inches. The circular entrance is often disguised by fallen leaves. In suitable areas these spiders congregate with a number of burrows in close vicinity to each other, but it is preferable to maintain them individually in captivity, as with all tarantulas.

Other Costa Rican species occasionally seen, although invariably more expensive than the Zebra, include the aptly-named **Costa Rican Panther Abdomen**

Tarantula (Metriopelma colorata) and the **Costa Rican Blue Front (Aphonopelma burica).** These are also burrowing species that need similar care to the Zebra.

Further south, two popular tarantulas are found in Chile. The **Chilean Rose** or **Red-back (Grammostola cala)** is like its **Chilean Pink Tarantula** relative **(Grammostola spathulata)** in color and fluffy in appearance. These species have become more widely appreciated by tarantula enthusiasts during recent years for their docile natures and attractive appearance. The pale brownish fluffy covering on the cephalothorax contrasts strongly with the rose-colored abdomen, with adult males showing the brightest coloration. (The Chilean Red-back should not be confused with an Australian spider also known as the Red-back (Latrodectus mactans), a type of black widow spider that has a deadly bite.)

The Chilean speces do differ somewhat in their habits, however, because the Chilean Rose is in fact a burrower by nature, whereas the Chilean Pink lives essentially on the surface, hiding away under suitable retreats. Both need to be kept

Grammostola burzaquensis *from Argentina. This male shows a character often visible in male tarantulas, a distinctly small abdomen.*

quite warm, at a temperature of about 80°F. Other tarantulas found in southern parts of South America include the relatively dull **Argentine Black (Grammostola iheringi),** which has identical requirements to the Chilean Rose.

The huge **Goliath Bird Spider (Theraphosa leblondi)** occurs further north. It is occasionally available but invariably commands a very high price (largely because of its 10-inch maximum leg span) and cannot be recommended for the novice tarantula seeker. It tends not to be an arboreal species, but wanders instead through the tropical forests where it occurs. A high degree of humidity and a warm environment, about 85°F, are required in order to maintain these spiders successfully.

While the New World tarantulas are generally most suitable as pets, showing less of a tendency to bite than those from other continents, other species are occasionally available, notably from specialist suppliers. The **Horned Baboon Spiders (Ceratogyrus species)** originate from Africa. These can also be burrowing in their habits. They tend to do best in fairly arid surroundings and are relatively costly to acquire in the first instance.

Theraphosa leblondi, *the Goliath Bird Spider, occasionally reaches leg expanses of 10 inches, but it is usually quite a bit smaller.*

Asiatic species sometimes imported include the **Asian Black Tarantula** or **Bird-eating Spider** *(Melopoeus albostriatus),* which appears to thrive at a relatively low temperature, around 72°F, and will tunnel into the substrate of its enclosure. The description of "bird-eater" is a misnomer, especially for this type of tarantula, but the popular term has fuelled the mythology that surrounds these large spiders. The terms "bird-eater" and "tarantula" still tend to be used interchangeably. This confusion over names also extends to the Asian tarantula known as the **Asian Zebra** *(Melopoeus minax),* which differs from the Costa Rican zebra sharing this common name. It appears to be a hardier species and thus can be kept at a lower temperature, around 72°F, but similarly shows a perference for burrowing into the floor covering of its enclosure.

Occasionally you may even see a large spider described as a tarantula that is in no way related to this group of mygalomorph spiders! It could well be one of the African *Nephila* species, sometimes known as Giant Orb-web Spiders or Silk Spiders. Apart from lacking the basic anatomical differences that set tarantulas apart from other species, these members of the family Araneidae actually build very large webs to catch their prey rather than proving to be actively predatory like tarantulas. The method of construction they use is fascinating to watch, although a spider is likely to spend as long as five hours preparing its web.

The Giant Orb-web Spiders require different accommodations than tarantulas, but they are not difficult to maintain and breed quite easily. Males are significantly smaller than their female counterparts in the case of *Nephila (Nephilengys) cruentata,* which is probably the most commonly available species, and are light brown in color, compared with the contrasting yellow and black markings of mature females. Originating in a tropical area, these spiders should be kept warm, but high humidity does not appear to be essential for their well-being. A beautiful species of *Nephila* is common in the eastern United States and might well prove adaptable to keeping in a terrarium.

Closeup of one of the orb-weaving spiders (shown is a species of the genus Tetragnatha) *in a defensive posture.*

The Tarantula Terrarium

Accommodations

Whatever species of spider you decide to obtain, you will also need to acquire the necessary components to house your pet correctly. Many people use a converted aquarium for the purpose, and this is frequently the cheapest available option. Those made of acrylic plastic are preferable to glass, being lighter and less easily damaged than glass aquaria. The size will depend to some extent on the species being kept, bearing in mind that tarantulas need to be housed separately and some are more active than others. An aquarium that is approximately 12 inches in length, depth, and height is satisfactory for small species or individuals, but a larger enclosure will certainly be required for tarantulas such as the Goliath, with its long leg span. It is also essential to acquire a secure hood for the tank, since these spiders are surprisingly powerful and determined and can push off a loose cover without difficulty.

Bear in mind also that you will need to keep the tarantula warm, at a temperature in excess of 70°F, so a heat source is also likely to be necessary unless the room temperature is kept continually at this level.

It may be better to

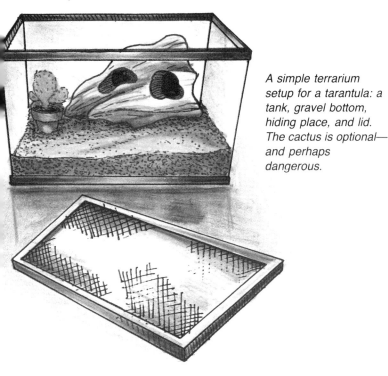

A simple terrarium setup for a tarantula: a tank, gravel bottom, hiding place, and lid. The cactus is optional—and perhaps dangerous.

Artificial rocks that can be made into many different landscaping configurations are available at pet shops and can create very interesting effects.

purchase a specially designed vivarium such as is used for housing reptiles. Attractive designs are available that incorporate a suitable cover plus a heat source. In some instances this will be set under thermostatic control, or a separate thermostat can be purchased and incorporated into the circuitry. Call in an electrician if you are worried about setting this up on your own if you wish to ensure there should be no faults in the system.

It is of course possible to purchase aquarium hoods to fit tanks of particular sizes, and these will often accommodate a light bulb that serves to warm the tank. Another conversion option is provided by a clear acrylic or glass sliding top with ventilation panels and a hole where a light fitting can be incorporated. A light bulb is preferable in this instance to a fluorescent tube since it will give off more heat.

Floor coverings

The floor covering of the tarantula's quarters should enable the spider to burrow if it is a species that normally excavates a retreat beneath the level of the substrate. Although soil may seem the obvious choice as a lining for

The gravel used in a tarantula terrarium doesn't have to be colorless; pet shops sell many different colors of gravel.

the tank, it is not recommended since it contains many potential disease-causing microorganisms. A more sterile substrate is to be preferred. Peat is favored by some tarantula keepers but can dry out rapidly and tends to become very dusty under these circumstances. Clean sand and even aquarium gravel are other possible options, especially for those species more likely to be found in arid surroundings in the wild.

A few commercial floor coverings are also available, and these tend to be more versatile than the previous possibilities. They can retain water effectively to maintain a humid environment for tropical forest species and are equally suitable for desert-dwelling tarantulas. Remember that although the tarantula tank will need little attention once it is set up, it will have to be cleaned out frequently if the substrate turns moldy, and such conditions are far from ideal for these spiders. In any event, an inert substrate is preferable to one containing a significant level of organic matter.

As a result, the commercial bedding materials are becoming increasingly popular. These may be based on volcanic lava rock, which is also significantly lighter than gravel or sand. Moving even large tanks is therefore easier if this is used as a floor covering. It looks attractive front of a window, since the sun's rays will cause the temperature within the tarantula's quarters to rise very rapidly to a fatal level. On top of a radiator or close-by is also not to be recommended, since this tends to result in a dry atmosphere being created within the tank. It is important to choose a location near an electrical outlet, moreover,

The best lid for a tarantula terrarium is one that is well ventilated but secure enough that the inhabitant cannot escape. Openings should be covered with gauze or foam.

and retains moisture well. Sufficient material to cover the floor of the tank to several inches in depth is required, especially for burrowing species.

Setting up the equipment
First you will need to decide where the tank will be positioned. Never set it in avoiding the need to trail extension cords around the room. Place the tank at a comfortable height to permit easy viewing by the whole family.

The tank should first be stood on a cloth as a precaution against scratching the underlying furniture, especially if it is made of glass rather than plastic. A commercial floor covering needs no preparation but can be simply tipped into the tank, whereas aquarium gravel will need to be washed off beforehand in a bucket, transferred to a colander, and then rinsed thoroughly under running water to remove debris. Surplus water should be allowed to drain off so it does not accumulate in the gravel and then stagnate in the bottom of the tank.

Although it does not appear essential to allow burrowing species to conceal themselves in the substrate it is preferable, so the floor covering should be several inches in depth. Part of the reason that tarantulas burrow is to survive in an arid environment, as distinct from concealing themselves from predators. Within the relatively cool confines of their burrows, water loss from their bodies is reduced and condensation provides a source of moisture that would otherwise be very difficult to obtain at ground level.

Water

In its enclosure, sometimes described as a tarantularium, the spider should have a source of water constantly available. This is best provided as a shallow container set in the substrate. In a relatively small tarantularium the clean plastic top off a coffee jar or a similar shallow vessel will prove ideal for this purpose. Place a layer of sponge in the

Tarantulas are fairly indifferent to plants, as long as they are not especially spiny or otherwise dangerous. They may dig up plants occasionally, but they never eat them.

Hiding places must be provided. These also help increase the humidity level around the resting tarantula.

water so that the spider can obtain fluid without difficulty but will not be able to drown in the container. The water bowl should be easily accessible so that the contents can be changed regularly. Evaporation of the water will also serve to increase the humidity within the tarantularium and thus contribute to the spider's environmental needs.

Decorating the tarantularium

The decor within the enclosure will need to be functional, yet should also be attractive. Tarantulas will appreciate retreats at ground level. Although rockwork can be used for this purpose, it must be positioned firmly in place, because if the spider dislodges it the block may fall on the tarantula with fatal

Both ceramic and wooden shelters are available that will fit into any terrarium and give the tarantula all the protection it needs.

The old standby and probably the simplest shelter for tarantulas—a flowerpot turned on its side. It is dark, durable, and cheap.

consequences. A safe rock hideout can be constructed using aquarium sealant. A flat area of rock such as a piece of slate will be required to form the roof, while two similar-sized rocks will be needed for the sides. The components can then be stuck in place using the special silicone-based sealant available from most pet stores.

The drawback of rockwork is its weight. Realistic lightweight substitutes are now often preferred by aquarists and are especially suitable for use in tarantulariums as they possess no sharp edges that could harm the spider. A further option that can be considered is cork bark. This is often stocked by florists and specialist reptile dealers. In the tarantularium it will serve as a retreat when placed on the floor, enabling

the spider to conceal itself beneath the inner curved surface of the bark.

While the inclusion of plants in the tarantula's quarters can be attractive, such decor is of little direct value to the spider. Be sure not to clutter the tank, as this will restrict the area available to the tarantula. Never include plants with sharp spines, such as cacti. These could fatally injure your pet if it accidentally becomes impaled. Although normally placid, a tarantula may move rapidly when under threat of being caught, for example, and could fail to avoid a cactus.

Any living plants incorporated into the tarantularium should be left set in their pots so the soil will not become mixed with the substrate of the enclosure. The pots can easily be disguised by the relatively deep floor covering. The plants themselves may help to increase the humidity within the tarantularium, especially if their leaves are misted regularly using a plant mister. If the ventilation is poor, they may tend to "damp off," with mold developing on the leaves. The environmental conditions must be improved under these circumstances, otherwise the tarantula will also suffer. In the humid environment of a tarantularium for Central American tarantulas, most plants will develop brown spots on the leaves and eventually die. Epiphytes such as bromeliads should be considered.

When keeping arboreal species of tarantula, notably the Pink-toed, further decor should be included within the tank so that the spider is able to climb and weave its web. The branches used must be

Since most tarantulas are nocturnal, they should not be left in nearly barren terrariums for long. Any such stress on a captive animal can result in illness.

fixed firmly in place so that they will not fall over. They will also need to be positioned with care so as to avoid the heat of the bulb in the lid of the tarantularium.

Lighting and heating

Tarantulas tend to avoid bright light, so a normal light bulb is unsuitable for use in their enclosure. In the relatively small confines of a tank, only a low wattage bulb will be required in any event. A colored bulb, such as a red or blue light, is to be recommended for this purpose (most spiders cannot detect red light). In a bigger setup, however, an infra-red heat source is probably preferable. Those of the dull emitter type produce heat only, rather than light, and will not be disturbing to the tarantula. Unfortunately, the majority of such infra-red sources are too powerful for the average tarantularium and are rather bulky, especially when fitted with a reflector shield around their base to concentrate the heat rays.

Some tarantula owners keep their pets at room temperature with no additional heat source. While tarantulas are relatively hardy and many can withstand temperatures below 70°F for short periods with no apparent ill-effects, this is certainly not to be recommended on a permanent basis. The tarantula's appetite declines under these circumstances when kept at a suboptimal temperature, and ultimately its health will suffer.

The temperature within the tarantularium can easily be monitored by means of a digital thermometer. These are widely used by aquarists and come in the form of a thin strip that simply sticks to the front of the tank and by color changes indicates the temperature within. If at all possible, set up the enclosure and monitor the temperature by this means prior to obtaining your tarantula. Any necessary adjustments to the thermostat setting are better carried out at this stage rather than when the tarantula has been introduced to its quarters.

If a light bulb is to be used as a heat source, it should be screened using a wire-mesh shield. There should then be little risk of the spider being burned since it will not be able to touch the light. In addition, ensure that the bulb does not dangle down within the enclosure, as this may attract an arboreal species to the cord, bringing it into closer contact with the bulb.

Because their soft abdomens burst easily if dropped, never give your pet a "ride" on your hand without supporting it.

Humidity

Apart from heat, the other major concern in the tarantula's environment will be humidity. Dehydration is probably the main cause of death in captive tarantulas, and for all species the aim should be to maintain a minimum relative humidity level of 70%. It is perhaps surprising that even tarantulas popularly regarded as occurring in arid parts of the world actually live in fairly humid surroundings. The contrast between nighttime and daytime temperatures causes condensation to form within their burrows.

The humidity level can be easily monitored within the tarantularium by means of an instrument known as a hygrometer. Calibrated in a percentage scale up to 100%, this piece of equipment is obtainable from most garden centers, hardware stores, and similar outlets. Unfortunately, hygrometers are stocked by few pet stores.

The provision of a water bowl will assist in raising the humidity, as will the presence of plants. Another option to consider is to include sphagnum moss, which can be lightly sprayed on a daily basis. A suitable covering can be placed in one part of the tarantularium where it is easily accessible for spraying purposes. The use of moss in this way will prevent the substrate itself from becoming saturated with water, while the fine droplets on the moss will evaporate quite readily, contributing to the overall humidity within the tarantularium. You can obtain packets of sphagnum moss from florists and from herpetological suppliers (it is a popular bedding material for amphibians).

Ventilation options

Ventilation is an important feature of the well-organized tarantularium. Although tarantulas often require humid conditions, they will not thrive in poorly ventilated surroundings where mold will flourish. This problem is less likely to be encountered when a low glass or plastic lid is used to provide the roof to the enclosure, as this has adequate ventilation panels incorporated into its design. The situation may not be as satisfactory if an aquarium hood covers the tarantularium. The sliding ventilation panels present in some hoods will need to be covered with mesh to prevent the tarantula from escaping should it gain access to the roof.

The bare patch on the abdomen indicates that this Red-leg likes to defend itself by spreading stinging hairs.

Hood problems

Most traditional aquarium hoods feature a "splash-shield" beneath the lighting fixtures so these will be protected from water. Used in the tarantularium, the splash-shield may permit the spider to climb out into the space between the shield and the hood where the bulb is located, since there is usually a hole in the shield for ventilation purposes. This access will have to be blocked off securely using 1/2" mesh wire. It should be taped firmly in position so that no loose cut ends of mesh are exposed, since these could injure the tarantula. Hoods with sealed lighting units are becoming more popular in aquaria and do not represent any hazard to a spider kept in the tank beneath, although they tend to operate using cool fluorescent tubes rather than warm tungsten bulbs.

If the light appears too bright, then affix a layer of colored paper on the outer surface of the plastic cover over the light, checking that it does not present any fire hazard here. A better option is to obtain a piece of red plastic sheeting, cut it to the appropriate size, and then fix

it firmly below the existing plastic cover to reduce the light intensity accordingly.

Other options

A variety of containers have been used, with varying degrees of success, for housing tarantulas. The converted aquarium is certainly the most versatile option. Components such as

Although this terrarium provides sufficient cover, the substrate will not allow digging of even the most simple burrow. Burrows allow the tarantula to live in very dry areas by increasing the humidity.

hoods are easily obtainable and compatible with the aquaria chosen. If desired, you can have a large tank accommodating several spiders simply by partitioning it using special dividers as used by fishkeepers. This provides an economical means of housing a number of tarantulas, as only one tank and hood will be required.

Plant propagators are favored by some enthusiasts but are really only suitable where no auxiliary heating is required. They can be set up in a similar way to a converted aquarium, although choose a design with mesh-covered ventilation holes rather than opening or sliding hatches in the roof for this purpose, so that there is no risk of the tarantula escaping. Sliding ventilation panels can be used if they are firmly taped in a partially opened position, but invariably the ventilation within the propagator will be compromised as a result.

Some propagators have heating elements within their bases, but these are likely to prove dangerous. The same applies to soil-warming cables. Tarantulas will burrow to escape heat, and yet since the heat source is actually in the bottom of the enclosure in the case of a propagator, the tarantula will simply become hotter, rather than cooler, when kept in this kind of accommodation. Soil-warming cables present a further hazard in that they present an obstruction to the tarantula's burrowing habits. They should not be used, especially in the quarters of burrowing species.

Various plastic carrying cages, complete with lids and often handles, are available from pet stores and sometimes are recommended for housing tarantulas.

Although they can be useful for transporting tarantulas and rearing young spiderlings, the majority are too small for housing adults on a permanent basis, and no heat source is available that can be used within such units. The only option, therefore, if the background temperature is too low is to position a lamp at a suitable height over these cages to provide additional warmth for the tarantulas.

Another possible way of accommodating a tarantula is in a plant dome, providing that you can maintain the temperature in the room at an adequate level. These domes are made of thin

Although not as readily available as tarantulas, scorpions are growing in popularity. Species with mild and harmless stings should be selected, such as this Pandinus imperator, *the giant West African Forest Scorpion.*

plastic and are relatively tall, so that they can be used for arboreal species if required. Entry is by means of a zipper, so there is no risk of a tarantula being able to escape by itself from this type of enclosure. Live plants can be incorporated within the dome, but the floor area can be rather small compared with more traditional ways of housing a tarantula in a converted aquarium.

Building an enclosure

For the enthusiast, it is possible to build a block of containers for tarantulas that also provide an inexpensive option when rearing spiderlings. Melamine-covered chipboard is ideal for the purpose since it can be easily cleaned when necessary and will not be adversely affected by conditions of high humidity. The joints should be sealed with aquarium sealant in order to exclude mites that may sometimes be introduced into the tarantula's quarters by insects used as food.

Alternatively, the chipboard can be made into a small cabinet with sliding panels either on the roof or at the front, depending on its positioning. Light fixtures can be located on the sides to provide heat. Individual covered rearing containers are placed within, forming a nursery unit that is relatively inexpensive to operate and easy to service, with all the tarantulas being readily accessible. The temperature is monitored by means of thermometers located close to the floor for accuracy, while a hygrometer will provide a reliable indication of the relative humidity level in the cabinet. Ventilation holes must of course be provided, with grills being most useful for this purpose. Apart from acting as a rearing unit, this kind of cabinet can also be used for a number of adult tarantulas if required.

Feeding Your Tarantula

Tarantulas are very easy to look after, providing that their environmental needs are met with regard to temperature and humidity. The newly acquired tarantula, especially an imported specimen, may be more demanding at first. Once the typical signs of dehydration, notably a sunken abdomen and an inert disposition, have been corrected, the tarantula will start to show an interest in food. There is no need to worry unduly if it fails to feed immediately, since in the wild these species are unlikely to feed every day.

Feeding

The way that food is presented determines to a certain extent whether it will be accepted by the tarantula. All tarantulas will take only animal prey and will show no interest in plant matter. They tend to ignore items that do not move and thus are inclined toward living prey, although they may be persuaded to take meat dangled on a piece of thread near them.

Tarantulas generally sense their prey by sound, detecting vibrations close by, rather than relying on sight to form a part of their hunting skills. It is certain that they also possess a sense of taste that may be linked to a scenting ability. Odors are important in many invertebrates, and much research is being carried out in the field of pheromones, which are chemical substances

Tarantulas tend to attack moving prey, so they will take dead food if it is gently waved before them on a string or slender straw.

A Curly-leg Tarantula (scientific name unknown) feeding on a cricket. The spider literally digests the cricket in its skin, leaving behind a shriveled husk.

produced by females which serve to attract potential mates. Female tarantulas may well produce pheromones, and the lyre organs, hairless spots on the underside of the legs around the joints, may act as scent detectors. Certainly tarantulas will reject some insects after catching them, notably beetles and cockroaches that have a bad odor or taste associated with them.

Tarantulas do not actually stalk their prey but tend to remain inert until it is within reach and then grab the unsuspecting creature, paralyzing it with their venom. Although in domestic surroundings invertebrates are likely to form the basis of the tarantula's diet, tarantulas occasionally feed on small vertebrates in the wild. They take small reptiles and may even capture young birds if the opportunity presents itself. This has given rise to their names "bird-eaters" and "bird-spiders," reflected in the scientific name of *Avicularia,* a generic name once applied to most tarantulas.

Grasshoppers are harder bodied than crickets and more difficult to buy and culture.

Feeding options

It is not difficult to supply a suitable diet for a captive tarantula, even in a highly urbanized area. The two basic options to consider are mealworms, which are actually the larval form of a meal beetle, and crickets, smaller versions of locusts. These livefoods can be easily obtained from your local pet store, from mail-order specialists, or sometimes even fishing bait sales.

Termites are available in tremendous quantities in some areas and provide excellent food for small tarantulas.

Mealworms

Mealworms are probably easier to keep than crickets and can be housed simply in a container such as a clean, empty plastic ice cream or sandwich box. Ventilation holes need to be punched in the lid, and the bottom of the container should be covered with a thick layer of chicken starter meal. Check that this does not contain any medical additives, notably drugs known as coccidostats, as these could prove harmful to the mealworms. If chicken meal is not easily obtainable, then bran, oatmeal, and corn meal can be used. These are stocked by grocery stores and health food stores but

Typical mealworms are quite hard-bodied beetle larvae. Although easy to culture and buy, it is best not to give them as the sole diet of your spider.

A typical mealworm culture contains larvae of various sizes and their shed skins.

Prepackaged oatmeal flakes have proven to be a very good growing medium that does not fungus rapidly.

Water should not be provided in a container housing mealworms. They get enough moisture from a small slice of apple placed on top of their food, into which they burrow. The apple will need to be changed at regular intervals as it dries up, but apart from this, there is no need to worry about the mealworms. The piece of apple must never be allowed to go moldy. They should be kept in a relatively cool environment, however, as this will slow their development down, making the larval stage last longer. Neither the almost inert pupae, which are whitish in color and much broader than the mealworms themselves, nor the black adult beetles seem as palatable to tarantulas as the yellow and brown larvae. Only a handful of larvae will be required each week by a tarantula, so a self-sustaining population is relatively easy to maintain successfully. Mealworms of different sizes are sometimes available from specialist livefood suppliers, with the giant forms being most suitable for larger tarantulas.

There is no unpleasant odor associated with the

tend to be less balanced in terms of nutritive value compared with chicken meal. This in turn can affect the feeding value of the mealworms, although nutritional disorders apparently are not recognized in tarantulas. If you are concerned about this possibility, however, and rely on feeding mealworms almost exclusively to your tarantula, then add a small quantity of a vitamin and mineral supplement to the bran and mix it in thoroughly to improve the food value.

culture of mealworms, and breeding necessitates no additional expenditure on equipment. For breeding puposes, however, the adult beetles should be transferred to warm surroundings, being maintained at a temperature of about 75°F. One of the advantages of breeding your own supply of mealworms is that smaller larvae than are usually commercially available can be obtained, which can be an invaluable plus when rearing young tarantulas.

Mealworm beetles lay eggs that can take about six weeks to hatch, so compared with some other invertebrates cultured as food their life-cycle is relatively lengthy. Indeed, it may take as long as four months to be completed. When required, the mealworms can be collected from the bran by placing a damp (*not wet*) cloth on the surface of the container and keeping it covered for a short time. The larvae will be drawn to the surface by the moisture and can be easily removed at this time.

One of the merits of mealworms as a food source for tarantulas is the fact that there is no risk of them injuring the spider, even if it chooses to ignore them. This is not necessarily true of crickets, which are another

A newly molted mealworm larva is paler than its companions and relatively soft-bodied, but it will harden within a few hours to a day.

widely available livefood. Unlike mealworms, which tend to be sold by weight, crickets usually are available only in larger numbers, and it may be difficult to acquire fewer than 50 at a time.

Tiny hatchlings tend to be rather small for fully grown tarantulas but can be very useful for spiderlings. It is possible to purchase a quantity of hatchling mealworms and then rear them through their molts into adults. The life cycle in this instance can take six weeks or longer to complete, and some degree of cannibalism is almost inevitable through this period.

Crickets

Crickets require more sophisticated housing than mealworms. It is possible to accommodate them in a converted aquarium heated with a light bulb to maintain the temperature in their quarters around 77°F and

Crickets are available at many pet shops and at virtually all bait shops. Their culture takes up quite a bit of room, so many keepers prefer to just buy what they need.

with a relative humidity reading around 70%. As with the tarantulas themselves, a shallow dish of water filled with sponge will help to maintain the humidity with no risk of the crickets drowning themselves. Apart from dry food such as oatmeal, the crickets will need to be offered grass on a regular basis. This should only be obtained from areas where no chemicals, especially pesticides, have been used. As an added precaution in case the grass has been fouled by animals, it should be washed thoroughly and shaken to remove surplus moisture before being given to the crickets.

Certainly in an urban area it may be better to grow your own supply of grass. This can be done quite easily using an empty margarine tub filled with peat. Bird seed, such as plain canary seed, can be sprinkled on the peat and thinly covered, with the container being transferred to a warm spot to enable germination to take place. Rather than watering the seeds during the early stages and probably flooding the container, spray the surface thoroughly using a plant mister each day. If the seed has been kept in the dark during the early stages, transfer the container to a window sill once germination is apparent. When the shoots are of a reasonable length, the container can then be transferred to the cricket accommodations. Several cultures can be started in succession to guarantee that a fresh supply of grass is constantly available to the crickets.

Special laboratory cages are produced for housing crickets as well as grasshoppers and include a container for egg-laying in the floor. Female crickets use their long ovipositor to bury their eggs directly in a pot of moist sand. Ideally, the container should be several inches in depth. Once the eggs have been laid, if the pot is removed to separate quarters and kept moist by daily spraying, the young crickets should start to hatch after about two weeks. Avoid mixing crickets of widely differing sizes, as the older individuals will prey on their smaller companions.

In order to facilitate catching the crickets, simply switch off the heat source and allow the temperature within the crickets' cage to fall, so they will become less active. Do not offer crickets that are bigger than the tarantula itself, minimizing the risk of the cricket injuring the spider. Grasshoppers, in view

Crickets can also be collected from the wilds of your back yard, but these may be contaminated with insecticides.

of their larger size, are potentially more dangerous in this regard, although they can be offered to bigger tarantulas. Keep a watchful eye on the spider at feeding time just to ensure that it is not threatened by its potential prey. Injury is most likely to be caused when the tarantula is about to molt, as it will become relatively inert and lose its appetite at this time.

Feeding arboreal tarantulas stick insects

Arboreal tarantulas present a particular challenge in that they are usually reluctant to descend to ground level in search of prey. Conventional invertebrates offered as food will often tend not to climb up branches in the cage. This certainly applies to mealworms, and generally to crickets as well. It is possible to feed the spider directly by placing such insects within its reach. Many arboreal tarantulas will readily retreat into a cardboard tube, as found in the center of kitchen toweling. This can be cut down in size and food items

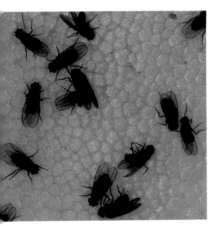

Fruitflies make excellent food for small tarantulas. Cultures are easily purchased and maintained, although they sometimes get a bit smelly.

placed within for the spider.
   As an alternative, an arboreal form of livefood can be offered, with walkingsticks or stick insects (phasmids) probably being most suitable for this purpose, as they are easy to keep and breed and have no smell associated with them. Culturing of flies is of course possible but proves an unpleasant procedure. There may be over 2,000 different species of stick insects, and they can range quite widely in size. The Indian walkingstick (*Carausius morosus*) is freely available, at least in Europe, and easy to maintain. In the U.S. other species can be collected or purchased from biological supply houses. Males of the Indian walkingstick are extremely rare and females reproduce on their own without mating, laying relatively large, brownish eggs that are somewhat reminiscent in appearance of seeds. These will probably take several months and possibly longer to hatch, with the young stick insects being miniature replicas of their parent. They will feed on a variety of greens such as bramble, although if this is not available privet may be used as a substitute. These stick insects tend not to be too sensitive with regard to temperature and will not require additional heat in the average room. When placed within the tarantula's enclosure, the walkingsticks will appear immobile at first and then will climb up the

branches, where they will be easily accessible to the spider. Suspending a piece of privet directly over the tarantula's retreat will serve as an added attraction to encourage the stick insects to move to this part of the tarantularium. Bramble is not recommended within the tarantularium because of its sharp thorns.

A varied diet
Although in the wild certain tarantulas do feed on vertebrates such as small lizards, there is really no need to offer these creatures to captive individuals. Similarly, although some owners offer day-old mice, known as pinkies, to large tarantulas that frequent the floor of their enclosure, this is not essential, nor do young birds have to be offered. Tarantulas are opportunistic feeders and will grab whatever is within reach. Offer plenty of variety within the invertebrates available, and your tarantula will remain in good health.

If you are concerned that there may be deficiencies in certain areas of your tarantula's diet, lightly sprinkle the prey with a general food supplement available from a pet store before offering the invertebrates to the tarantula.

Depending on the tarantula's feeding habits, it may gain some benefit by this means. Alternatively, obtain a soluble supplement that can be added to the drinking water. A separate dish containing the solution can be incorporated into the tarantularium in addition to the usual water source for about a day every two weeks. The use of a supplement may be of particular value close to a molt, when the tarantula is more likely to be debilitated.

Many insects that you can collect at lights at night or with a net in your back yard are suitable as tarantula food. Soft-bodied types are preferred.

Feeding principles

The actual food consumption will vary according to the individual. Under normal circumstances, the average tarantula may consume perhaps half a dozen crickets during the course of a week. Unlike mealworms, these will not attempt to bury themselves in the floor of their enclosure. Watch your pet's feeding habits and do not supply a large number of invertebrates at one time, but offer a maximum of three or four and replace these as they are eaten. It is also advisable, certainly for crickets, to place some oatmeal in one part of the tarantularium. They will then be able to feed and are less likely to attack the tarantula as a result.

Mealworms can present more of a problem, as they tend to be less conspicuous. It is possible to confine them in a dish containing a very shallow covering of bran or chicken meal, with the dish itself being set into the substrate of the enclosure. The tarantula may need to be shown to this spot, but should soon come to feed here readily. Alternatively, you can let the mealworms roam free in the tarantularium, but they may rapidly become inaccessible to the spider.

A shrunken abdomen on a tarantula is usually a sign that it is not feeding, but a small abdomen isn't necessarily a bad sign . . . the specimen could be a male. This Curly-leg Tarantula seems perfectly healthy.

Handling and Bites

Handling a tarantula

Sooner or later it will be necessary to handle your tarantula, but routine handling is not really to be recommended, as there is always the possibility that you may drop the spider, causing it severe if not fatal injury in the process. If you are nervous, it is preferable to wear a thin pair of gloves so that if the tarantula does attempt to bite, you will not drop it in fear.

Tarantulas seem to vary in can also be a factor to consider—indeed, the Goliath Bird Spider is certainly one of the harder species to pick up without difficulty. Although they may appear sluggish much of the time, tarantulas under threat of being picked up can prove especially agile.

The most straightforward means of lifting the spider is to hold its cephalothorax, using the thumb and first finger positioned between the second and third pairs of legs. It is important to try to

*How **not** to handle your tarantula! This specimen could easily bite if annoyed or surprised, and its stinging hairs are sure to get into the skin of the hand that is holding it.*

temperament, with the North American species generally proving most docile. Those from other parts of the world may be more aggressive. Those capable of stridulation, producing the characteristic hissing sound by using their chelicerae and pedipalps, can prove especially disconcerting to handle. Size

lift the tarantula directly upward so that it suddenly loses contact with its environment. This will cause it to become disconcerted by the sudden absence of sensory input from its surroundings, and it then should not attempt to struggle to free itself. If the tarantula actually makes contact with the sides of its enclosure while being lifted out, then it will certainly use its legs to try to escape, but do not tighten your grip. Just ensure that the spider is firmly and adequately restrained and transfer it to another container without delay.

It is of course possible to move a tarantula without having to handle it directly. Simply encourage it to move into what it considers to be a retreat, such as a cup introduced to its enclosure, gently using a pen to direct it along the desired path. Then, with a piece of perforated card or screening placed over the top of the cup to keep the tarantula secure within, the spider can safely be transferred.

Some owners delight in allowing their pet to walk over them, but this can prove hazardous both for the handler and the tarantula. In the first instance, you can encourage a tarantula to step onto your open hand and lift it out of the tank in this way, but take great care to ensure that the spider does not slip out of your grasp onto the floor, as this may well be fatal for the tarantula. Keep your other hand close beneath so that it can act as a safety net should the tarantula move off your hand while it is being

carried. Similarly, the spider may then return to the original hand, and the process will probably need to be repeated yet again. There is really little merit in moving your tarantula by this means, and it is certainly more hazardous than actually lifting it up directly.

The tarantula's hairs
Always take care when handling a tarantula and you should not be bitten by your pet. The tarantula may choose to defend itself by other means first. It may rub a number of the hairs from its back, using its hind legs for this pupose. These can cause severe irritation and may even cause temporary blindness if they enter the eys of predators. For this reason never hold a tarantula close to your face, since this form of defense is favored by many species kept as pets, including the Mexican Red-leg. Also avoid allowing a tarantula to walk over your arm: this can give rise to a rash caused by the contact of the urticating hairs with the skin. When a tarantula has shed its hairs, this will result in a bald patch being evident on its abdomen. These hairs will be replaced, but check for the bald patch when purchasing tarantulas, since a bald abdomen is often a

feature of an old individual nearing the end of its life span.

The tarantula's bite

The fearsome reputation of the tarantula's bite is simply not justified, although as with the venom of insects such as wasps and bees its effects can be severe in a very few people who prove allergic to it. Tarantulas generally give an indication of their intention to bite before actually doing so. They will raise their bodies, support themselves on their hind legs, and show their mouthparts. They will then lunge forward, stabbing the victim with their fangs, though which the venom is injected.

The actual effects of a tarantula bite appear to vary but rarely cause any real discomfort. The pain and discomfort may not be as great as that typically associated with a bee sting, although some swelling and reddening of the site is likely to be apparent. There is also likely to be some throbbing where the fangs punctured the skin. Treat the wound as for insect bites and seek medical advice without delay if you believe that you could be allergic to the venom or if other symptoms, such as nausea, develop. In the vast majority of cases, recovery

from a bite is uneventful; indeed, the tarantula may not actually inject venom in every instance.

There is no evidence to show that any tarantula owner has succumbed after being bitten by his pet. The likelihood of contracting rabies from a family dog would thus seem to be

If you must pick up your tarantula, be sure the fingers are not placed near the fangs. Bites may not be dangerous, but they can be painful.

greater than that of dying from a tarantula bite—both are exceedingly unlikely. In any case, there is no need to handle your tarantula directly under normal circumstances, even when moving it out of its usual accommodations.

Other Aspects of Care

Daily care

Tarantulas are remarkably undemanding pets. Their food supply should be checked daily and the water vessel replenished as required. Daily spraying to retain the humidity reading at the desired figure may also be required, but apart from these simple tasks there is no need to worry about cleaning out the tarantularium. The fecal matter excreted by tarantulas dries very rapidly, is totally odorless, and only small quantities are voided. Mummified cricket bodies may have to be removed, but the tarantularium usually can be left undisturbed for as long as a year before being given a thorough cleaning.

Spiders are very subject to death from small quantities of insecticides—all insecticides, including those in pet care products. Be careful!

FLEA & TICK
SHAMPOO
FORMULA
FOR DOGS

When the unit is cleaned out, simply replace the substrate, having transferred the tarantula to temporary yet secure accommodations.

Threats to your tarantula

Unsuspected dangers may be present within your home that could prove fatal to your pet. For example, never pick up a tarantula after handling tobacco unless you have washed your hands thoroughly, since nicotine is one of the most potent natural insecticides and contact will invariably prove fatal for tarantulas. Smoking will also liberate nicotine from tobacco, and this is equally likely to be fatal close to a tarantula.

Avoid using fly sprays and insecticide strips in the home. The aerosol droplets and vapor can spread from one room to another, and the concentration may be sufficient to kill your tarantula. Anti-flea preparations used on other pets, notably cats and dogs, are likely to have a similar effect. Use such chemicals out of doors, away from the tarantula's surroundings.

In an emergency situation you may be able to protect your tarantula from poisons by moving it out to a safe locality sealed in a large plastic bag within its enclosure. There is unlikely to be any effective treatment available if it does encounter a poison, but minimizing exposure will afford the tarantula some hope of survival. Poisoning through the food chain should be considered. For this reason, never offer invertebrates that may themselves have been exposed to pesticides.

old outer exoskeleton to be replaced ultimately by a larger, new body covering.

Several distinct phases occur during this process, starting with the premolt, which heralds the onset of the molting period. At this stage the tarantula loses its appetite and physical changes occur within its body, with calcium being

A tarantula with its body held off the ground is usually angry and becomes unpredictable. Think of it as a growling dog and be cautious.

Molting

The molting phase is always a worrying period for tarantula owners. During its molt the spider even may be wrongly assumed to have died as it lies on its back. Molting is, however, an essential part of the tarantula's development. As it grows, its restraining exoskeleton becomes too small. The molt enables the

transferred to the body organs from the exoskeleton that will shortly be shed; here this vital mineral is stored on a temporary basis. There is no need to worry about the tarantula's refusal to feed during the molt. Some can in fact survive for as long as two years without feeding, although water must be constantly available. (Of course, this is no excuse to starve your pet.)

A behavioral change may also be apparent at this time: tarantulas often kill prey prior to a molt but then refuse to eat the bodies. Clearly, under these circumstances no new food should be given until after the spider has replaced its exoskeleton, when it will start to feed rapaciously. Fluid intake is also likely to then increase again, as it did just before the molt.

Immediately prior to shedding its existing exoskeleton, the tarantula is likely to construct a web, especially if it is undergoing its first molt in captivity. Once the spider is established in captivity, this aspect of molting behavior tends to be lost. The tarantula, instead of lying on this "molting cradle," simply rolls to its back on the floor of its enclosure.

The separation of the old exoskeleton results from fluid being secreted into the gap between the old and the underlying new body covering. Once on its back, the tarantula's existing exoskeleton gradually splits, and slowly the spider escapes from this constraint as the molting phase progresses. The length of time for the molt to occur can be variable, but it is unlikely to be less than 12 hours. On emerging from its shed skin the tarantula appears smaller than it was beforehand, but during the next stage, described as the postmolt, the new exoskeleton expands in size. It is reinforced by the calcium previously stored in the body organs.

The inner covering of the alimentary tract, extending to the pumping stomach, is also shed and replaced during the molt. It is for this reason that the tarantula will refuse food throughout this period. Indeed, the end of the molt is indicated by the rekindling of the spider's appetite.

The time between active molting periods, described as the intermolt phase, varies depending on the age and sex of the tarantula. Young individuals molt more frequently than their older counterparts, shedding about every three months on average during the first two years of life. The intermolt period then becomes longer, extending to six-month intervals from this point onward until maturity. From then on the tarantula will only shed its exoskeleton on an annual basis. Overall, males tend to molt less frequently than their female counterparts.

Always avoid handling a tarantula that is about to molt or has recently molted.

The molted skin of a tarantula is of course the spitting image of its owner. The newly molted tarantula is usually distinctly more colorful and appealing than it was before molting.

During the premolt phase it may appear darker in overall coloration. Once the exoskeleton has been shed, the soft body of the tarantula renders it very vulnerable to injury or predators, and while it is on its back the spider is effectively defenseless.

While a fit, healthy tarantula passes through the molt without difficulty, an old or sickly individual may succumb, especially if it is unable to escape entirely from its old exoskeleton. As a guide, the actual shedding should take no more than a day, with the tarantula lifting itself off its back within a few hours of emerging from its former protective casing.

Exhibiting tarantulas

After a molt, the tarantula will have a totally new exoskeleton. Even hairs lost from the abdomen will have been replaced. This is the condition in which some owners like to exhibit their pets. Although at present there are apparently no specialist shows for tarantulas, they may be shown in mixed shows where other animals are also entered. It tends to be necessary to include tarantulas in the more unusual classes. Take your pet in a container such as a box with clear plastic sides and a handle on the lid so that it can be easily viewed.

Do not encourage handling by curious onlookers, who are unlikely to be familiar with the correct way to restrain tarantulas and could easily drop your entry as a result.

Breeding Your Tarantulas

Considerable strides have been made in the breeding of tarantulas under captive conditions during recent years, but much still remains to be learned about the reproductive behavior and needs of many species. The individual hobbyist can make a significant contribution in this field, noting any breeding attempts and relevant points of interest such as temperature, humidity, and the layout of the tarantularium, as well as the diet being offered to the spiders. The actual system of introducing the male and female to each other may vary, and as always, a degree of luck will be required to encourage these large spiders to breed successfully in the home.

The end of each pedipalp of a male tarantula bears a process that is usually black and somewhat pointed. This is used to transfer sperm to the female.

Mating

Sexing usually involves recognizing males. The pedipalps on the front of the cephalothorax serve as the sex organs in the male tarantula and end in the palpal bulbs. Males are usually smaller than females and have hooks on the femurs of their first legs. The testes are located within the abdomen. The ovaries of the female are of course also internal. The genital apertures in both sexes are found in the middle of the epigastric furrow, which is an indentation on the abdomen connecting the two book lungs closest to the cephalothorax.

Conditioning plays an important part in successful breeding. For example, tarantulas kept at a suboptimal temperature will, not suprisingly, show little interest in breeding. In terms of housing, a partitioned aquarium setup is ideal for housing a pair, with the male's quarters being well padded on the floor with a thick layer of sphagnum moss. In his ardor, once he is aware of the female, the male tarantula often becomes extremely active and may well attempt to climb up the sides of the tank, falling backward onto the base of the tarantularium, where the bed of moss serves to reduce the risk of injury. For this reason, breeding tanks should not be taller than 12 inches.

When assessing potential breeding stock, be sure that the spinnerets of males, located at the rear of the abdomen, are fully intact. Without these the spider will not be able to weave its sperm web, which is vital for the successful transfer of spermatozoa directly onto this silken web, and then, having emerged from the web, proceeds to crawl to the top. Next, using the enlarged pedipalps, the male reaches back into the web and absorbs the ejaculate into his palpal bulbs.

The production of a sperm web is not dependent on the presence of a female tarantula. Most males weave

Although female tarantulas tend to stay near their burrows, males may wander miles away from home in search of females. The short-lived males are easier to find and thus end up on the market more often than females.

spermatozoa from the genital opening to the pedipalps and thus to the female tarantula.

The sperm web is rather like a tent and usually is woven at least in part against the glass, regardless of the decor within the tarantularium. The male tarantula produces the ejaculate containing the a web of this type within a few weeks of their adult molt. It may not be very conspicuous, and only the remnants may be visible in the tarantularium. The web is usually destroyed soon after it has been used, although male tarantulas do vary in this respect. Even if a web is not seen, it could well be worthwhile to attempt to use the male for breeding purposes. The short life span of male tarantulas means that, in any event, for serious breeding attempts you should have more than one male of any species available.

There appears to be no set breeding period for tarantulas, but they should not be mated close to the start of a molt. The female stores the spermatozoa in the organs known as spermathecae, and these, along with their contents, are lost every time the tarantula molts her exoskeleton. Both members of a potential pair should be well-fed prior to a mating encounter to increase the likelihood of success. A male will then be full of vigor, and the female will display less of a tendency to be aggressive, not being so tempted to regard her potential suitor as a meal!

In the wild, many male tarantulas go in search of females, thus it is usual to introduce a male into a female's domain. This should only be carried out under close supervision so that the combatants can be separated if necessary before a fatal blow is inflicted. Do not place the spiders directly together, but place the male near the female.

Under normal circumstances, the male will soon display in the female's presence by vibrating his legs. She may decide to respond in a similar fashion. Then, perhaps after being touched by the male, she stands with her front legs held off the ground and her fangs open. The male now seizes her fangs with the mating hooks present on his femurs and, using his pedipalps, rhythmically strokes the underside of her body, which appears to induce a trance-like state. Once this stage is reached, mating can follow quite safely. Each male palpal bulb containing spermatozoa is then inserted in turn into the female's genital aperture.

The male now withdraws rapidly and should be removed without delay from the female's quarters. After mating, the female is likely to become aggressive toward her partner if permitted the opportunity to do so. In the wilds this problem does not arise as the male can escape without difficulty. Have a piece of stout card to hand so that if the female does suddenly attack she can be separated from the male without too much difficulty, the card serving as a temporary divider while the male is lifted out by hand and returned to a separate container. It is certainly not true that female tarantulas kill their mates routinely after mating, unlike certain spiders in which this practice is common even in the wild.

While just one mating can give rise to fertile eggs, it may be preferable for several successive matings to take place using different males, hoping that at least one is mature and has recently completed a sperm web.

There appear to be slight differences in the mating patterns of the various the case of arboreal tarantulas, such as the Pink-toed, it is believed that females have a more active role in the courtship procedure compared with terrestrial species.

Egg-laying

Although mating takes place, fertilization of the eggs does not actually occur until perhaps several months later, when the spermatozoa are released from storage in the genital pouch (seminal receptacle). Since the pouch

As more tarantulas are bred in captivity there should be less pressure put on populations of the more desirable species such as the Mexican Red-leg. If at all possible, try to get pairs of your tarantula species and try your hand at breeding them. Success is not that common, but it is becoming a less rare occurrence.

species, although these are at present not well-documented. It is therefore worthwhile making notes on the breeding behavior of tarantulas in your collection. These may one day add to the existing knowledge in this field, which still tends to be rather sparse, even for commonly kept species. In and its contents are shed along with the exoskeleton, if the female molts after mating but before egg-laying the sperm are lost. Preparations for egg-laying commence with the preparation of a cocoon in which the female hides herself. Having enmeshed herself in her silk casing, she then proceeds to weave a further area of silk on which the eggs are laid. The number of eggs in a single brood will vary according to the species concerned, but over 500 is not necessarily unusual, and more may be laid on occasion.

The silk where the eggs were produced is then rolled up to form a structure described as the egg sac, which is watched over by the female tarantula while her young are developing within. Never introduce a male, or indeed any other tarantula, to a female with an egg sac, as she is certain to attack them under these circumstances. Indeed, she should be left alone as much as possible throughout this period, since there is always a risk that the egg sac could become damaged, with fatal consequences for the developing spiderlings within.

Hatching and rearing
Ensure that humidity is maintained within the tarantularium throughout the developmental period, which can last for nine weeks or even longer, again apparently depending to some extent on the species concerned. When the young tarantulas do emerge from the egg sac (or ootheca, as it is sometimes more technically described)

they are often white in color until their first molt, although clearly recognizable as spiders. The female should be taken away from her brood shortly after they hatch, otherwise she is likely to start eating them. The young spiderlings could be removed instead, but this is a more difficult task in view of their minute size and will cause more disturbance to the female in any event.

Since a single brood may total hundreds of young tarantulas, this in itself presents problems concerning rearing. At first they can be fed small insects, such as hatchling crickets or wingless fruitflies. Fruitflies are a popular livefood with aquarists and are easily cultured, provided that they are kept warm. They can be obtained in the form of a starter culture from some pet shops and dealers that advertise in aquarium magazines. They are also readily available from biolgical supply companies, which can supply the culture medium necessary for raising the flies. This is most conveniently obtained in the form of a powder that is simply made up with water to yield a paste. Other mixtures based on sugar and even banana skins, if replenished on a regular basis, will serve to sustain a breeding population of fruitflies.

The cultures themselves should be started a couple of weeks after the egg sac is formed so that there will be a good supply of fruitflies for rearing the spiderlings if the containers are kept warm, around 72°F. The wingless form of the fruitfly is preferable since they are not able to fly and are thus easier for the young tarantulas to capture.

Within a few weeks, however, the spiderlings will start to consume each other, leading to a dramatic fall in their numbers unless they are transferred to individual containers. Rearing the great number of hatchlings that can result from a single egg sac is not practical unless you have a very extensive area available to you, such as a specially heated and equipped nursery room for the spiderlings. Breeders often favor small jars for housing young tarantulas, with suitable ventilation holes (screened over to prevent escapes) being punched in the lid. Partitioned cages can be used, these being fitted into the confines of a special cabinet for the best possible utilization of space. Offer food of the appropriate size, giving larger invertebrates as the spiderlings grow.

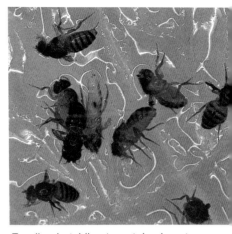

Feeding hatchling tarantulas is not easy, as sufficiently small food may be hard to find. Vestigial-winged fruitflies are excellent.

Molting by the young

Molting occurs even before the young tarantulas have left the protective cocoon of their egg sac. The tiny spiderlings may lose their white coloration after the first molt. Further molts follow at progressively longer intervals. Great care must be taken at these crucial points in the lives of the young tarantulas. Their growth rate will be slowed if they are kept at a suboptimal temperature, and molting difficulties are more likely to be encountered under these conditions, especially if the relative humidity is also low. The length of time normally taken for the tarantula to reach its adult size is influenced by these factors and also depends to some extent on the species involved, with tropical tarantulas attaining maturity quicker than those from other parts of the world as a general rule.

The appetite of young tarantulas is quite variable, depending on the frequencies of their molts. It is thus important to keep them well-fed to see them through these periods of self-enforced starvation with minimum side-effects. Losses will be inevitable during the rearing period and also occur in the wild. (In the wild, fewer than 0.5% of newly hatched tarantulas may survive to reproduce successfully.) It may be possible to sell them cheaply as youngsters to fellow enthusiasts, which should mean that more can be reared successfully.

Hatching the eggs artificially

Under normal circumstances, the female tarantula guards her egg sac closely, moving it within the burrow to the best position for optimal temperature and humidity. In captivity, however, some females become excessively nervous and may destroy the egg sac and the developing brood. In certain cases this may be traced back to excessive interference on the part of the owner or to a lack

of suitable cover in the tarantularium. For this reason it may prove worthwhile to put in the cage a small bottomless box with an entry hole cut into one of the sides, where the female can retreat, excavating a chamber within.

There has recently been growing interest in hatching young tarantulas artificially. This is quite feasible, although it is still recommended that the female be allowed to look after the egg sac through the initial phase of the incubation process. The temperature and humidity within the enclosure are vital and should agree with that required for the adults of the species. Excessive humidity with poor ventilation is likely to prove harmful, as this will almost certainly cause the egg sac to turn moldy. As sterile an environment as possible is therefore recommended from the outset, so for this reason soil should not be included within the hatching unit.

Development of the eggs takes place within the egg sac, giving rise to the white "nymph" stage. It is important to turn the egg sac daily, as the female tarantula would do naturally. While in this form, losses are likely to be at their highest among the young spiders. Certain

If you live in an area where tarantulas are naturally common, such as the American Southwest, you may have more luck breeding the local species. This is because the climate does not deviate from what the spider is used to in nature, meaning less stress on the specimen. This is Eurypelma californicus.

species leave the egg sac at a more advanced state of development than others, but after a period of eight weeks the egg sac should be carefully slit to produce a hole through which the young tarantulas can escape. This minimizes the risk of cannibalism and also serves to prevent spiderlings becoming trapped within the egg sac, as can happen if it is attacked by mold. A variety of materials can be used to construct an artificial egg sac if required, but do not use any sticky adhesive tape that might trap the spiderlings. Either stitch or staple the ends and sides as required, placing the young spiderlings within. Once the spiderlings are several weeks old, they will then need to be transferred to separate accommodations to prevent excessive losses through cannibalism, as in the case of their naturally hatched counterparts.

Tarantula Ailments

As with their breeding habits, much remains to be discovered about tarantula ailments. The environmental conditions are vital, however, in ensuring that your tarantula remains healthy and feeds well. Watch closely for signs of a problem. For example, if your pet insists on attempting to immerse itself in its water container, this is almost certainly an indicator that the humidity within the enclosure is too low. Since captive tarantulas tend to lead solitary lives, there is little risk of disease being spread directly from one specimen to another.

Fungus

The significance of bacteria and viruses in tarantula illnesses is not well-documented. Certainly fungi will attack and kill tarantulas, and their origins are frequently traced back to poor environmental conditions. The first step is obviously to improve the tarantula's environment and then to attempt to carefully wipe off the signs of mold evident on the body. It may be worthwhile using an anti-fungal medication (available at pet shops) on the affected area. There is always a danger that the fungus may actually gain access to the interior of the tarantula's body, which invariably proves fatal, so rapid treatment is required to prevent its spread.

Injuries

Probably the most common and serious injuries encountered in tarantulas result from falls. This may even happen within the tarantularium if the spider climbs up the side and falls awkwardly onto a projection beneath. Damage to the exoskeleton is more likely to arise during the molt, as the outer covering will be softer than normal at this stage. Loss of hemolymph is a truly life-threatening situation for the tarantula and needs rapid attention. Various methods may be used, depending on individual circumstances. The immediate action taken must be to stem the flow of hemolymph from the site of injury. This may be achieved using tissue paper applied to the wound, but unfortunately it usually is not possible to plaster the injury by conventional means because of the tarantula's bristles. Success has also been claimed by adding various substances, such as flour, directly to the wound, which may encourage clotting of the hemolymph.

Even if the immediate first-aid measures prove

A tarantula's legs can be its downfall. Each leg has at least six major joints, each of which can easily break and leak body fluids. Multiply this by eight legs and two pedipalps and you can see the problem. Fortunately, tarantulas are able to regenerate lost limbs.

successful, there is a likelihood that there will be persistent seepage from the wound. It may be possible to repair the damage to the exoskeleton using dental cement carefully applied over the area of injury. It might even be possible (but very unlikely) to find a veterinarian who will undertake stitching of the wound using absorbable sutures.

Injuries of this type on the legs are less severe and should heal without the need for radical treatment. Actual loss of a limb can in fact prove a life-saving procedure for a tarantula. They may even remove an injured limb themselves. Tarantulas and other spiders possess leg joints specially adapted for this purpose to minimize loss of hemolymph. The sealable joint is located at the junction of the coxa and trochanter. If pressure is applied to a limb, this is the point of least resistance, and thus the distal portion will be shed, while a diaphragm present within this particular joint covers the break, stemming the flow of hemolymph, which rapidly clots. This means of defense is one reason why tarantulas should never be restrained, even on a temporary basis, by their legs. The loss of a leg is not a serious handicap to a tarantula, however, and provided that it lives long enough a replacement will be generated over successive molts.

Molting difficulties
It is worth obtaining a bottle of glycerin just in case your tarantula encounters difficulties during its molt. Under normal circumstances no assistance will be necessary, but if it does not free itself easily, make up a solution of glycerin using a teaspoon of glycerin to two cupsful of tapwater that has been allowed to stand for awhile to reach room temperature. Then, using a plant sprayer or preferably an eyedropper, trickle the solution carefully over the tarantula, taking care not to clog the book lungs with fluid. For this reason it may be worth standing the tarantula on rigid plastic plant mesh so that it can be sprayed directly from beneath as well as from above, since it will be lying on its back. Keep it moist. The glycerin solution should serve

to soften the spider's rigid outer skin adequately within a few hours so that it can free itself. Avoid touching the exoskeleton directly, although as a final resort, if after prolonged treatment with the glycerin solution no improvement is noticeable, you may try to remove the body covering very carefully using a pair of blunt-ended forceps. There is always a risk of damaging the new tissue beneath, precipitating a critical loss of hemolymph.

Do not be surprised if your tarantula refuses to feed for a number of weeks after a problematical molt. It may well be having difficulty in shedding the lining of the upper part of its digestive tract down to the pumping stomach. This is not so crucial, since tarantulas can survive for months without food, provided they have eaten well beforehand. Ensure that the humidity within the tarantularium is kept high to assist the spider in shedding its digestive lining, and this problem should resolve itself spontaneously. Under normal circumstances, once the molt is completed the spider's appetite often returns within just four or five days.

It is not uncommon for some hemolymph to escape from the leg joints during a

The giant wasps known as tarantula hawks or tarantula killers are often a tarantula's worst enemy. The sting of the wasp paralyzes the spider long enough for the wasp to lay an egg on its abdomen. The tarantula then becomes a living food locker for the growing wasp larva.

molt, and this need not be a cause for concern. It is inadvisable to handle your tarantula directly for about two weeks after a molt, as this could lead to serious injury if the exoskeleton has not hardened properly.

Parasites

The best-known parasites (more properly they are specialized predators) of tarantulas are the hawk or spider-hunting wasps belonging to the family Pompilidae. These relatively small creatures appear to be one of the tarantula's major predators in the wild. As the wasp approaches the spider, the tarantula will rear up in an attempt to deter the aggressor, but the speed of the wasp usually permits it to strike without difficulty. It seizes the tarantula's soft underparts and injects a deadly poison that rapidly paralyzes its victim. The wasp then proceeds to drag the spider into a suitable burrow. The final stage in this grisly process entails the laying of an egg by the wasp on the spider's abdomen. Once the larva of the wasp hatches, it begins to consume the tarantula lying alive but paralyzed in the earth.

On occasion, tarantulas with various fly larvae in their abdomens are sometimes offered for sale. The most common sign of this infestation is likely to be a misshapen, often slightly swollen abdomen, coupled with inertia on the part of the spider concerned. There is no means of dealing with this problem safely, and such tarantulas should not be purchased.

On rare occasions other parasites have been noted in tarantulas, including mites and small flies belonging to the family Phoridae. It may be possible to remove these safely by dabbing them very carefully with petroleum jelly applied using a cottom swab. Take care to ensure that there is no risk of blocking the tarantula's book lungs with this treatment, as this could prove highly counterproductive. Do not use insecticidal strips or treatments of any kind under these circumstances, as these are also likely to prove fatal for your pet.

Suggested Reading

THE WORLD OF VENOMOUS ANIMALS
By Dr. Marcos A. Freiberg and Jerry G. Walls
ISBN 0-87666-567-9
TFH H-1068

Contents: Introduction: Acknowledgments; Jellyfishes and Allies; Sea Urchins and Starfishes; Molluscs; Worms; Fishes; Introduction to Venomous Arthropods; Scorpions; Spiders; Dangerous Insects; Amphibians; Gila Monsters and Beaded Lizards; Introduction to Venomous Snakes; Rear-fangs; Cobras and Their Allies; True Vipers; Pit Vipers; Duck-billed Platypuses and Insectivores; Poison Control Centers; Further Reading; Index.
Audience: Venomous animals certainly aren't very pleasant, but they're unquestionably among the most interesting animals around— and as the fabulous full-color photos in this exciting new book prove, they're also among the most colorful and beautifully patterned. Covers many, many different groups, not just the commonly recognized ones, and provides practical information about each.
8½ x 11"; 192 pages
Illustrated with over 100 full-color photos

ALL ABOUT TARANTULAS
By Dale Lund
ISBN 0-87666-909-7
PS-749

Contents: The Tarantula As A Pet. What is A Tarantula? The Anatomy. Selecting Your Tarantula. Housing. Feeding. Water. The Bite. Training. Moulting. Breeding Ailments. Conclusion.
Audience: For anyone who likes tarantulas and would like to have one as a pet, this book offers very practical advice about keeping your pet alive and in good health for many years.
Soft cover, 5½ x 8', 96 pages
Contains full-color photos

TARANTULAS
By John G. Browning
ISBN 0-87666-931-3
KW-075

Contents: Tarantulas in General. Choosing Your Tarantula. Keeping Your Tarantula Healthy. Breeding Your Tarantula. Tarantulas and Human Culture. Exhibiting Tarantulas.
Audience: Highly practical, this book is an excellent combination of sensible advice and fascinating good reading; you don't even need to own a tarantula in order to enjoy it. It tells everything you need to know and then some.
Hard cover, 5½ x 8½", 96 pages
32 full-color photos, 22 black and white photos and line drawings

The World of
Venomous
Animals
Dr. Marcos Freiberg
and Jerry G. Walls

Index

A gorgeous specimen of the Mexican Red-leg Tarantula, Brachypelma smithi, the species favored by many keepers.

CO-024 S

t.f.h.

TARANTULAS

A COMPLETE INTRODUCTION

Brachypelma smithi, *the colorful Mexican Red-leg Tarantula, is a docile species that has introduced many keepers to the hobby.*